11 PILLARS OF CONFIDENCE

Build & Lead an Empowered YOU

By
Arthur J. Rutledge

LA Tribune Publishing

Table of Contents

About the Author

Author, entrepreneur, Vertical mindset and leadership speaker/coach Arthur j. Rutledge was born in Detroit, Michigan and currently resides in New York City. He's a John C. Maxwell [JMT] certified coach, Speaker, Coach & Trainer. Executive Contributor for Brainz Magazine, his mission as a vertical mindset &  servant leadership speaker-coach-trainer is to support people on their daily journey to reach higher levels, to take off in purpose, and to build emotional intelligence to overcome life's transitions/challenges.

His love of people leads him to connect others to what it is to move forward confidently and to give step-by-step encouragement to reach unforeseeable heights. As a compassionate leader and a connector, he likes to interact with people. He is determined to build a legacy that will be responsible for the evolution of global intentional awareness, abundant living and to inculcate interdependency in the world. Further, Arthur is the co-founder of People's Pride Shoes. He and designer/ CEO Carlyle Hanson have fabricated a footwear collection of which their mantra, "Take pride in what you wear."

Arthur is the host of the inspirational IGTV discussion with leaders in various industries about manifesting their dreams. Arthur uses the mantra, "Beam with your dream by putting fire on your desire… with confidence and perseverance, fulfillment is yours to have."

Foreword
by Kevin McGovern

Confidence is that intangible and most desirable state of mind to which we strive so ardently. We all know it takes consistent effort and often seeks reinforcement, but most of all it's generated from within as we build our foundation of confidence in and to our lives and others.

My early life was also filled with daunting adversity. At the age of 12, I became the man in my family as my dad died when I was 11, my mother was handicapped and lived in bed and my brothers were off in college. I secured 3 jobs including 150 daily papers to deliver. Although I didn't have a bedroom I had a very nice couch to sleep on at night. Many nights I studied out on the fire escape with my flashlight when my sister wanted to watch TV. I did well in HS which I paid for and earned an academic scholarship to Cornell where I'm still active as Trustee Emeritus. It changed my life!

As scholarships were not available for law school I decided with my inner confidence / can do attitude to enroll in full time law school even though I only had enough money for my first semester. I worked over 55 hours a week and went full time to law school at St John's, a really good training. I found out that 3rd yr tuition would be covered if I could become Editor in Chief of the Law Journal. So with that inner confidence and strength got that done as well.

I could go on with some other life accomplishments but I simply wanted to show evidence that confidence can conquer our personal mountains ! **As I say to so many young** people : YOU can achieve the impossible, you simply have to break it down and achieve possible steps ! Remember the more you carry the stronger you get !

Arthur Rutledge personally rose from daunting adversity to which I can certainly relate. I often say the more you carry the stronger you get. Yes, building confidence is work well spent but the kind of work that as we build our momentum seems less and less burdensome and becomes truly inspiring and productive.

This book is loaded with nuggets of wisdom and tools from Arthur and many of our foremost scholars to successfully confront our challenges and build fortified confidence in ourselves. As Stephen Covey's book "Seven Habits of Highly Effective People "changed my life when I read it 1992 (it's still on my kitchen counter for periodic reference) Arthur's 11 Pillars of Confidence can, if you open your mind, heart and soul, truly change your life.

For me, my life's ultimate goal is internal harmony and affecting the same to others. A primary manifestation of that extraordinary state is inner and outer confidence.

Enjoy the read and build your harmony with inner and outer confidence to all of you !!

Introduction

What do you want most in life, and I don't mean material things?

What's the reason you achieve most of what you set out to accomplish?

What inspires you, or who inspires you, to reach new heights?

What ideas are you cultivating to achieve your mental, personal, or career goals?

Why haven't you found solutions to these questions?

Is it low self-esteem?

Poor self-values?

Broken confidence?

Feeling breathless with self-doubts?

Are you filled with feelings that leave you uninspired, feeling like you're falling backwards instead of adopting the constructive attitude of learning from the lessons of falling forward?

This book will give you the support you need to free up those pathways, enabling you to breathe easier and gain a clearer understanding of how to elevate your confidence from flat to zapped!

Our ideas need nourishments to grow precise & impactful ... repetition with time will multiply & then abide to abound.

At the age of 11, I attended 7th and 8th grades at Detroit's Nolan Elementary Middle School. It marked a significant moment in my life, one filled with both excitement and fear – perhaps the most intense mix of emotions I had ever experienced.

Actually, scratch that – it was the second most intense. At 8 years old, I vividly recall the summer camp at the YWCA, where I learned how to swim. Stepping into the public school system from the smaller world of private schooling at M.I.C.D. Academy (Michigan Institute for Child Development) was a big leap. Looking back, I realize that Rosalyn Murray, our principal, was one of the best I've ever known, though I didn't fully appreciate her at the time.

Spending six years, from first grade through sixth grade, at M.I.C.D. Academy taught me how to express myself and expand my horizons. It was there that I learned to trust myself and embrace exploration. Yet, like any kid, I longed to be like the others on my block and attend public school. After relentless pleading with my mother, she reluctantly made my wish come true – a testament to the persistence of children everywhere.

However, my transition to Nolan Elementary Middle School was far from smooth. I found myself trying to catch up with and seek validation from the school's seasoned veterans, who had known each other since elementary school. Being the outsider, I disturbed the established order, and unfortunately, that didn't sit well with the cliques. The result? Bullying.

Growing up on a block in the hood, I was always considered the odd one out. I was the kid who wore a uniform with a crossbow tie for six years, the one whose mother would yell his name just before the street lights came on, and the one who had to stay indoors until she got home from work out of fear for my safety. I even had my toys stolen by kids I thought were friends but turned out to be anything but.

Facing middle school and reliving that sense of isolation was a disheartening experience. At the age of 11, when I was most impressionable, my self-esteem could have easily led me down the wrong path in life. Thankfully, it didn't.

During that turbulent time in my life, amidst the chaos, there were classes – after all, that's what school is truly for. It was in one of those classes, my first geography class with Ms. Bledsoe, that my understanding of where I was expanded into where I could go. Ms. Bledsoe had a remarkable way of opening up the world right before my eyes.

Now, I don't know if you're familiar with Sagittarius, but we're known for our love of travel. Ms. Bledsoe ignited that passion within me. In my imagination, I saw myself as a combination of James Bond, Waldo, and Isaac from The Love Boat. Yes, Isaac was the man back then – serving up good advice with a great attitude while traveling the world with a supportive crew. What more could I have wanted at that time?

By the time I finished 7th grade, I caught a glimpse of the person I could become. I daydreamed about visiting those exotic locales Ms. Bledsoe had introduced me to. Though my primary dream at that age was to become a professional dancer, have endless fun, and, of course, impress the ladies, I also grappled with a realization: Could I actually achieve those dreams, and how long would it take?

It was exhilarating to think about the possibilities, but I couldn't shake the feeling of being alone in my aspirations. None of my friends shared my excitement for world travel – in fact, none of them had even ventured outside the Midwest.

These thoughts, along with others of a similar nature, consumed my mind. But amidst the uncertainty, one thing was clear: I vowed to myself that I would embark on those worldly adventures one day.

Due to the optimal option, where optimism becomes contagious through believing in your best outcome, we choose to persevere or make things happen because there is no other choice. It's not a matter of do or die; it's a commitment to do and dedicate. Eventually, things improve as we cling to hope and surround ourselves with others who hold high hopes for us.

You have the power to create or discover your best future self by aligning your desires with your confidence. Without confidence, you cannot achieve your best life.

In this book, my sincerest hope is to raise awareness of lapses in inner faith, despite the numerous mistakes that may have led you to complacency in what you already have or expect from life.

The courageous live and die well. If you find yourself in a state of spiritual stagnation, don't worry—it's time to resurrect you to the living.

In writing this book, I found myself frequently needing to take my own advice. It involved a lot of self-love, pacing, trust, and establishing a routine to which I held myself accountable. These aspects of the process were crucial and hard-earned moments, especially during the darkest times. Without intentional focus and decisive action, these moments could erode the good I sought to do.

My belief in why I am here and my vision of the greatness within each of us kept me going. I made confidence in my ally a long time ago. However, I didn't always recognize my own value. While I had values, without understanding your own worth as a person deserving of the best, those values can become misplaced, leading us down the wrong path in life. This book is part of my mission to consciously shape and sharpen how you perceive yourselves, to support and activate the aspects of you that were left behind on the playground as a child – the dreamer, the ally, the confidant, the action-taker, the unique and unbounded spirit.

Every action taken since that time has diminished, like a lamp being turned down for the night to rest. Every day can feel like that when we're depleted from lack of action in our lives. This is what happens when a dream is deferred or defeated. Lack of confidence can hinder our potential, keeping us from where we're meant to be. We are beings meant for more than most realize. The adventurous child within us knows this, and I'm certain that person seeks the best in us several times a day – in work that could be better, in friendships that could be more enjoyable, and in those moments of discouragement when we wonder, "What's going on with us?"

Throughout this book, we will explore these stories and obstacles as we delve deeper into conversations of compassion with confidence. We'll provide actionable content and introduce encouraging instructions that will help make the process of building your confidence consistent.

Additionally, we'll delve into how relationships foster trust through our commitment to ourselves. Speaking of commitment, during those 11th and 12th-grade years, I learned four invaluable lessons that helped me overcome some of life's toughest challenges: self-trust, self-respect, self-reliance, and seeking wise advice. I believe these qualities reside within you as well, and here, we'll work on transforming your inner child into the person you are capable of becoming today.

"Are you driving your life forward or is life pulling you along."

– Zack Friedman.

People often ask me, "Why are you so focused on mindset and the behavior of others?" My response is simple: it's because these are the only aspects of our lives that we can truly control. When we can align our mindset and behavior correctly, we open the door to greater fulfillment and progression in life.

To prepare for anything life throws our way, we must make it a practice. Life isn't just a series of random events; it requires careful consideration and planning. Just like preparing for a journey in a car, we need to clear our minds, establish our primary destination, and focus on reaching that goal. We also need to adjust our seats for comfort and, most importantly, fasten our seatbelts for safety.

Although these steps may seem routine, they reflect a conscious decision to prioritize our safety and well-being during our travels. Overthinking before embarking on a journey can lead to delays or complications, making the trip more challenging than anticipated. Conversely, failing to give sufficient thought or consideration to our actions can also have negative consequences.

If you find yourself caught in a cycle of negativity, it's essential to step back and reassess your approach. Instead of resigning yourself to a challenging journey, strive for a smoother ride by focusing on positivity and proactive decision-making.

These examples are not exaggerated, they do illustrate how we often approach our experiences without fully considering the potential consequences of failing to switch our mindset (M) before shifting into drive (D). Christian evangelist Charles R. Swindoll famously asserted, "Life is 10 percent what happens to you and 90 percent how you react to it." The right mindset is what happens within you during that crucial 90 percent. This level of self-evaluation requires both awareness and confidence.

In Jonathan Rauch's book "The Happiness Curve," he quotes, "The river alters the voyager, not just the scenery. Although the world beyond the bend in the river looks less exciting without an overlay of realist optimism, it does not look emptier or narrower. It looks richer and deeper... That is the beginning of wisdom." Self-belief is a brave inner attribute that gives us strength during the harshest conditions. When a storm rages, both land and sea endure its fury. In the midst of the tempest, time can seem to stretch on indefinitely. We're all too familiar with the destructive power of nature. Yet, as the storm passes, the land begins to heal. The soil settles, making way for new vegetation. Trees stretch out their branches toward the sun, and delicate flowers thrust upwards in a field. The sea, stirred and shaken, purges portions of pollution from its waters, revealing its effulgent beauty, mirroring the clear skies above. The sun dances its light gracefully on the surface of the tides as they ebb and flow. These are the convictions, communications, and confidences of nature. All of nature is faithful in the little things.

Confidence is a remarkable attribute. It enables us to navigate life with grace and self-assurance, tackling challenges that might otherwise seem insurmountable. Yet, confidence is also capricious. Some individuals exude it effortlessly, sometimes bordering on overconfidence or arrogance. Others struggle to find confidence and can become self-conscious, whether in social settings, the workplace, or other aspects of daily life.

Essayist and poet Christopher Morley once remarked that in his adventures in the workforce, he realized that accomplishments are defined by individuals, not society. Self-awareness can illuminate our unique sense of success.

Low confidence can result from various factors, ranging from our genetic makeup to our life experiences. While extremely low self-esteem is concerning, a lack of confidence isn't always negative; some research suggests it can foster success by promoting hard work, self-reflection, and receptivity to feedback. Nevertheless, many of us yearn for a bit more courage and certainty as we navigate life's challenges.

"There is a morning inside you waiting to burst forth into light."

– Rumi

Let's delve into what it takes to unleash that inner light at will. Discovering these successes can empower you to share your radiance, inspiring others towards meaningful change, courage, and confidence.

11 pillars of confidence is not only a book on confidence. It's learning how excellent we can be with the right nudges and correction points. To hold tight to our commitments and renew our integrity to what we say we will do matters more than we think. It's also a reminder of what courage lies beneath, behind, side and inside us. The quintessential parts that get to be whole in our endeavors to properly rise in the worthiness it takes to know fulfillment. Furthermore, it will support you in finding what it takes to feel in harmony with self-value in our pursuit of prosperity during our journey. I'm excited to drive Awareness that can lead to Agile thinking. This book is about cultivating confidence and all its attributes to lay down a highway self-trust. To see that loving courage inside of yourself is enough to enable the inspired will to get through past down thinking and open authentic communication with yourself and others. To enable life that's possibly if not surely laid dormant for way too long. These chapters will empower you to leave the mundane behind and realize how reachable is the sublime. You get to secure a truth that Behooves you to consciously move forward despite folly. To continuously rise to the occasion by constructing a process of trustworthiness in yourself. If you have not stepped into a mindset for internal fulfillment then I want this book to be a fertile and nourishing time to begin. We essentially grow strong in the weak places & gain wisdom through our evaluated experiences of win and lose.

"Now faith is the substance of things hoped for, the evidence of things not seen."

Hebrews 11:1

I believe in your potential & your being open to the possibilities of what you can manifest after embracing the ideas you will be reading. My underlined agenda is to get you so highly confident That it will create a tipping point of compassionate interdependence, enlightenment & empowerment. If I can get enough of you to put your attention on the same intentions, the world can tilt in the same direction of hope. Yes, hope is an action along with patience. Both are very powerful when combined. Moreover, those only work when we have self-belief that we can do what we desire and the faith that we will!

Getting yourself to an open-minded state of being will take the tools I put in this book and practice with repetition. The possibilities of what can be learned here is priceless. So take notes and notice the thoughts that have slowed down and corrected so thoughts that just ain't so. We have pages for that at the end of every chapter. If you need more space, get more papers or clear some memory in that tablet. Do the work to get the reward. This is your life and time to start living it well now! Commitment to the process of your growth together.

When you shine, I shine. Together let's shine!

CHAPTER ONE

Start with Confidence

"Don't speak negatively about yourself, even as a joke. Your body doesn't know the difference. Words are energy and they cast spells, that's why it's called spelling. Change the way you speak about yourself, and you can change your life."

— Bruce Lee

Confidence that gets observed gets acted upon.

— Arthur J Rutledge

A confident mind thrives on creativity, while a competitive mindset can often hinder or even stagnate the creative flow that yearns to be unleashed. Creativity is versatile, adapting to meeting you wherever you are and capable of taking you to unimaginable heights. Cultivating self-empathy is key to maintaining patience and nurturing a creative mindset. Remember, your creativity knows no bounds when nurtured with kindness towards yourself.

Empathy Confidence boosters:

- Self-affirming Words (pdf adjectives)
- Self-efficacy talk comes from good decisions or accomplishments of the past.
- Self-trust by doing something new to get good at a daily task that's a routine.
- Self-ease better attitudes about things by consciously producing new ideas and suggestions that are light, simple, or fun when having negative thoughts throughout the day. Creativity is in us, we just left it dominant with our inner child. Believe me, it's awaiting your summoning the rod of remembrance.

"Never go to sleep without a request to your subconscious."

– Thomas Edison

Your mind possesses immense power, capable of influencing both your waking and sleeping moments. Assert your belief in this power by trusting that it resides within you, ready to manifest your desires. Embrace the conviction that you are prepared to receive success in any endeavor you pursue.

Instead of being resistant, learn how to be irresistible.

"The invariable mark of wisdom is to see the miraculous in the common."

– Ralph Waldo Emerson

"Let they who would move the world first move themselves"

– Socrates

Reflecting on my life, I recognize moments of confidence in certain areas and moments of unconscious doubt in others.

One method I employed to access a more authentic version of myself was by using the acronym **T.A.P**, which served as a reminder that most endeavors require three essential processes to succeed:

- Temperance
- Attracts
- Perseverance

Understand what it means to be brave & courageous. (Be bored or be bold and life's an adventure!)

- It takes a loving patience to be kind to ourselves. We are brave each and every day by just living, and staying in the fight and living your best life. (Confidence: finding & creating the best in us!)

- Reflect on all the good things we did today, acts of bravery, kindness, etc. (Confidence: finding & creating the best in us!)
- Be bold to speak your opinion/mind/story and be patient in building skills of empathy and compassion to better connect your authentic self with those around you (Joining the process of we to achieve!)
- Communication (Work in progress or joining the process of we to achieve!)
- A majority of life is communication with another person! Both spoken and unspoken (Intuitive)
- Miscommunication happens when we lack emotional intelligence and become reactive rather than consciously act
- Learn to listen and take notes on feedback to know if your message is getting across
- Know your audience and interests to create subject matter that connects with you (Logical, Emotional, Existential, Musical, Naturalistic personality types etc.)
- Less is more
- Dogs are able to communicate to us without speaking emphasizing the unspoken subconscious of language that is felt
- Our brains are vast and like computers computing and absorbing data we have a learner's mindset (Curiosity) and proper attitude (optimism and enthusiasm).

- The root of communication is commune. Commune means community, collaboration, coming together. Knowing this is the root of communication, what we can give to one another, giving our input, our experience, our stories help us serve in being a servant leader.
- Grow vocabulary to deliver ideas better
- Sincere interactions build trust, always give the heart before the hand.
- Love Language and Self Communication

"One important key to success is self-confidence. An important key to self-confidence is preparation."

– Arthur Ashe

I have often said that the chance you crave is in the belief you make. Confidence is a confirmation of us being here & relishing the rewards in life for being beautiful and unique.

Without societal conditioning or deliberate intentionality in affirming our identities, many aspects of life as we know them wouldn't exist. People wouldn't dance, seek connection with others, believe in themselves, practice self-forgiveness, act selflessly, pursue fulfilling careers, or recognize the value inherent in living.

Growing up in a bustling city like Detroit aka Motor City, often leads to constant self-doubt at every turn. I frequently found myself needing to reinforce the significance of my dreams. One of the primary ways I achieved this was by nurturing focused ideas. It required consistent practice and attentive self-questioning. What was my inner child guiding me to pursue? Why did I struggle to remain on a single path? How could I distinguish myself in my own life?

If you find yourself grappling with similar internal inquiries while navigating your life's journey, then you're on the right path. I'm reminded of Lao Tzu's wisdom: "The journey of a thousand miles begins with a single step." These questions propelled me forward, one step at a time, fostering optimism and self-understanding along the way.

In Viktor Frankl's "Man's Search for Meaning," he explores the profound concept that personal growth is not something that can be quantified externally but rather is deeply intertwined with our intentional pursuit of it.

The strength of our confidence directly impacts the traction our desires gain. When our confidence is robust, our aspirations are propelled forward with greater force. Conversely, if our personal growth is left on autopilot, with little attention to who is guiding the wheel, a collision is bound to occur.

In leadership roles, the task of enhancing confidence can seem daunting. Therefore, it is crucial to provide reassuring doses of calmness when approaching the challenge of leading ourselves and others toward achieving their best results.

Below are four ways to invigorate and initiate healthy conversation around our attitudes related to confidence:

You can even ask yourself "What's my **P.H.A.S.E** today?"

Personalize - put your name on it. You have to claim it to achieve it!

Hypothesize - let your imagination "what if it works rather than what if it doesn't.

Analysis - stretch yourself to see self through different eyes. Away from judging ourselves…kindly & loving eyes.

Synchronize - attitude attune with mind, spirit, body… frequency alignment.

Emphasize - "Visualization process" stating present to holding in the mind & keeping it fresh.

> *"The object of art is to give life a shape".*
> *A Midsummer Nights Dream*
>
> *– William Shakespeare*

Give your life shape, color, texture and contrast. Practice giving the beautiful thoughts in your mind wings so not only to raise above mediocre expectations but so that your ideas can always transcend obscurity. These beautiful thoughts that gain you higher ground make you able to distance yourself from others' lack of vision.

In James Allen book, As a Man Thinketh, The Thoughtless, the Ignorant, and Indolent, seeing only the apparent effects of things and not the things themselves, talk of law, of fortune, and chance. Seeing a man grow rich, they say, "How lucky He is!" Observing another become intellectual they exclaim, "How highly favored he is!" And noting the saintly character and wide influence of another, they remark, "How chance aids him at every turn!"

They don't see the trials and failures and the struggles which these men have voluntarily encountered in order to gain their experience; have no knowledge of the sacrifices they have made, of the undaunted efforts they have put forth, of the faith they have exercised, that they might overcome the apparently insurmountable, and realize the vision of their heart. They do not know the darkness and the heart aches; they only see the light and the Joy, and they call it luck; do not see the longing arduous journey, but only behold the pleasant goal, and call it "good fortune"; do not understand The process but only perceive the Result, & call it chance.

> *"Self-true is the song that reminds me that my self-talk should be true to myself and to be true to others."*
>
> *– Arthur J. Rutledge*

> *"Through confidence, I've learned how to trust myself while making mistakes to persevere in the decisions that are not."*

– Arthur J. Rutledge

In my personal experience Personal experience when you observe something that sticks out because it is out of place, **T.U.C.K.It**

Transform

Uncertainty

into

Calm

Knowing

Possessing a strong sense of who you are and what you are capable of can carry you a long way in reaching your goals. Taking on a difficult task while full of self-doubt and pessimism often leads to failure.

"With confidence you have won before you have started. If you have no confidence in self, you are twice defeated in the race of life."

– Marcus Garvey

Feelings & Thoughts

CHAPTER TWO

Meet Your Dreams Everyday

"Make your future dream a present fact, by assuming the feeling of the wish fulfilled."
~Wayne W. Dyer

"Until one acknowledges the genius within oneself, one will have great difficulty recognizing it in others."
~David R. Hawkins

"Dreams are ours to inspire deeply & aspire higher".
– Arthur J. Rutledge

"When you dare to take on your dreams then you Will understand the magnitude of how far you have come."
– Arthur J Rutledge

Have you decided on a direction in life?

Have family or friends told you what things they think you are good at?

Do you know what your gifts, talents, or strengths are yet?

These and other questions about qualities that you may or may not have been important for identifying how effective you are going to be in pursuing your desires or dreams. It's always good to have curiosity when discovering who you are or what you love doing.

I can't remember a time in my life when I didn't know what excited me.

My first passion was becoming a dancer. The hip-hop new jack style of dancing of the 80s & 90s was my jam! Rehearsing in my backyard with friends in my early to mid-teens! Dancing battles against people in the neighborhood and high school dances. Two of our best rivals were Fred and Ant.

Although I never saw them practicing, the results couldn't lie. When Fred & Ant would show their moves, they were so tight! They put a fire in our belly to better ourselves every time we dance battled against each other.

I learned dreams can be sharpened if I'm willing to sharpen them.

My "why" became clear and that made me try harder and harder.

Somewhere along the way in life, you forgot your power and, in part, felt helpless in your pursuits as an adult. The good news is you can regain that type of confidence! Our dream stayed intact not just because we were good at dancing, not just because it was fun or a light distraction, but because we had learned lessons through facing challenges. To know if your dream is real, it needs to be challenged. Furthermore, we need to have a healthy relationship with these challenges. The challenges produce the confidence needed to endure the bumps on the head that will be encountered while obtaining your dream. It helps us to have a good attitude toward everything we want in life.

The right attitude will allow us to be proactive with our lessons. We become stronger learners through these lessons for our best lives. Add up your lessons and count your achievements. A practice in controlling your attitude is allowing yourself to face your fears as it prepares you to be stronger during your struggles. We should never stop doing what we love and be bold with our endeavors!

I've been involved in many teams and organizations, some organized, some not so much. One of the most crucial aspects of leadership is keeping the vision alive and in constant motion. "Nisus" is a Greek word defined as the mental or physical effort to attain a specific goal; it involves pains, strain, and striving, as well as a tendency to go with our impulses in whatever we are working towards. I believe the best way to be confident and creative with a vision or dream is to break the word down and then set your intention to stay strong with your nisus effort. I have put this acronym in place to help gauge whether you are on course to meet your dream daily.

Strike your dreams with might!

-**WORDS** are the one thing that God says have the power of life or death. Your confidence will always shrink to the level you are at, so practicing raising your energy is proportionate to what we say and how we say things to ourselves. Replace your negative words with positive ones daily. This doesn't have to be in the form of affirmations; simply staying mindful and catching yourself when doing it is important. To keep track of this, write on a specific calendar. You can title it "Getting Confident" or "Hands Up if You're Sure" like the commercial! Claiming your confirmed confidence dry and secure, lol! On this calendar, mark how many times you did the "word contest" every day for 33 days. I will talk more about this in the next word, "R" for Responsibility! Be kind to yourself if it feels like a roller coaster at first and in the middle of the 33 days. Facing resistance will happen during any change in life. This is no different. When you complete these 33 days, you will have a "D" for Dedicated on your Chest! Sometimes it can take longer. So, what! It's your life! Go another 33 days! You will feel the shift and feel the connection to your confidence.

-**IMAGINATION** is intrinsic and intricate to our connection from the hidden into the tangible. Your "why" in life is directly made real with an idea. Your idea is a new space where exploration takes place and your experience takes form, like the carbon that makes your steel become will! The energy of your will to make your desires materialize through a committed decision happens through sheer determination and self-belief. It's the knowing that you are worthy of achieving all you are excited about in life. One thing to shape our future: we must control our creative mind. Just like above, words of encouragement and disciplined action will work. "I've always been compelled by the idea that your mind, when you're asleep, can create a world that it perceives simultaneously: you've literally created a world in your dream... That, to me, has always been the most profound demonstration of the infinite potential of the human mind," said British-American filmmaker Christopher Nolan. Your infinite potential is calling for you! I mention in the other chapter how the ego shouts while the soul whispers. You are profoundly and uniquely you. Know the voice inside has a certain that's waiting for you to pull back and let free all that is in your heart to do.

"Imagination is a force that can actually manifest a reality. Don't put limitations on yourself. Others will do that for you," said Canadian filmmaker James Cameron.

Action step:

Whatever you can imagine that makes you feel lively and/or connected to what you would like to do in life, write it down. I had a client before who told me, "I don't like to write." In the immortal words of the old Dwayne Johnson character "the Rock" would say, "It doesn't matter"! If you want to "strike with might" your confidence, Rock Your Writing! In 33 days, you will get better at it. If you are a professional journalist, this will be different from your usual journalistic musings.

Your journaling has become average at this point. It's time to shake it up with the new intention of accelerating your hopes, aspirations, and dreams in a stretchy type of way.

On May 17, 2022, Dr. Saurabh Mehrotra on Neurosciences wrote an article "What Is the Memory Capacity of a Human Brain?" in medanta.org, stating that the memory capacity of a human brain was testified to be equal to 2.5 petabytes of memory capacity.

A "petabyte" means 1024 terabytes or a million gigabytes, so the average adult human brain can accumulate the equivalent of 2.5 million gigabytes of memory. That's a lot, yo! We have to start somewhere with endless endeavors to get our thoughts from strangers to relatives. Writing, reading, communicating, and collaborating will support in getting our imaginations out of stuck to drive sooner rather than later.

Learning accountability now will serve you greatly in the discipline and self-discussions you will have while relearning your childlike potential. In these 33 days, it's paramount to believe your learning is earning your confidence. "Stretching to improve ourselves should be the aspiration and can make living an adventure," my own personal quote.

-**EMOTION** as we know, can be extemporaneous, and so is the impact of imagination. Filmmaker and screenwriter Ava DuVernay asserts, "Creativity is an energy. It's a precious energy, and it's something to be protected. A lot of people take for granted that they're a creative person, but I know from experience, feeling it in myself, it is magic; it is energy. And it can't be taken for granted." This viewpoint of hers is so true!

I love the term emotional intelligence because when I hear it, I'm reminded that I can have self-respect for my intelligence. No matter what intelligence it is, I can make it work for me whenever I'm ready. So can you!

Self-trust is one of the keys in establishing what makes up emotional intelligence or EQ. For example, when I went back on my word for the umpteenth time, I chipped away at another piece of my mind's eye of integrity.

Birthdays, New Year's resolutions, commitments to family members, weight loss plans down the drain, asking for promotions that didn't happen, attempting to spend more time to achieve some semblance of quality of life that didn't work out, the list goes on and on.

This timorousness is a breakdown in character and seeps into every aspect of our lives. You get to take command and believe in yourself again. It's never too late to work on our intrinsic locus of control.

Knowing what we can control is as important as knowing what works for us in our lives. The awareness that you are the cause of all your dreams coming true is a confidence booster.

If you're in an external locus of control, then it is quite easy to feel that everything is happening to you. One path leads to acceptance and accountability, the other leads to despair in an attitude of suppressing and projecting tendencies. Just know that the decisions you practice become duplicates.

Guess what!?

Thirty-three days of this will support you in the self-trust process as well. Being honest with yourself, no matter how tough it might seem, do it anyway! To get this hammer time, you get to take on mirror time, facing those emotions in front of your eyes. Trust me, I will have future workshops around this and am available for coherent and constructive questions via DM/emails.

In the meantime, breathe, hug yourself constantly, speak plainly with yourself, and write down your experiences daily. Your dream is wonderful and waiting for you to know you are worthy. Use the following tool for **D.R.E.A.M.**

D for Dedication

Are you taking the necessary steps to make sure you are passionate towards your dreams?

Do you fall short on things you say you want to accomplish regularly?

Do you feel confident in who you are enough to achieve things you say you want?

If you haven't asked yourself these or similar questions, then self-doubt might be pervasive in the story that you have constructed in your consciousness. I've had negative self-thought patterns every time I attempted the things I desired. I found that only from persisting in little actions of my words, emotions, and imagination was I able to strike dedication with might.

R is for Responsibility

Responsibility is the state or fact of having a duty to deal with something or having control over someone. However, Webster's dictionary offers a rather lackluster definition. Responsible individuals rely on self-respect to maintain integrity by making the right decisions and taking appropriate actions. Owning up to mistakes is a mark of responsibility, whereas blaming is unproductive, especially in situations beyond one's control, which many human behaviors fall into. This phenomenon can be termed the "what we think we know but just isn't so" syndrome. As a side note, this is one reason why I'm quick to forgive both myself and others in my life. The realm of the unknown is infinite, which is why we must practice being responsible and accountable for our own lives.

In my youth, my attitude toward life wasn't as composed, and my emotions weren't in check. This lack of self-awareness led to self-centered behavior, perpetual tardiness, and a disregard for others' time, despite my great potential. I didn't value myself enough and often acted recklessly and impulsively. Confidence fluctuated frequently, a consequence of not facing myself enough and allowing misplaced desires to dictate my actions. Neglecting our integrity and trusting in our insecurities can be detrimental.

Thankfully, I had good leadership and a strong sense of self, thanks to my strong mother, a resilient church background, and some insightful friendships and mentors. It's essential not to let unknowns linger like a specter over our heads. Constant guilt can drive anyone haywire. Instead, love yourself and embrace the process of learning from past mistakes. Being responsible enhances our discipline, helps us plan our dreams with focus and integrity, and teaches us the importance of setting boundaries.

Even in the face of blame, judgments, and cynicism from others who refuse to take responsibility for themselves, forgiveness is key. "Concern yourself more with accepting responsibility than with assigning blame. Let the possibilities inspire you more than the obstacles discourage you," wisely said Ralph Marston. The greatest responsibility lies in honoring your word and actions to yourself and others. Manage this, and your dreams will receive all the support they need. As British Prime Minister Winston Churchill maintained, "The price of greatness is responsibility." Make your dreams a priority and treat your responsibilities with the maturity they deserve.

E is for Education

Education is a great avenue to bolster our dreams by honing our skills and nurturing our abilities. A great teacher is one who lives from their passion. In my opinion, achieving this requires curiosity, commitment, communication, creativity, and community. Through curiosity, we cultivate patience; through commitment, we foster perseverance; through communication, we imbibe values like vulnerability, trust, and connection; through creativity, we embrace agility and openness of expression; and through community, we develop compassion, generosity, and gain counsel.

These attributes will all contribute to the realization of your dreams and foster self-belief along the way. "Character is higher than intellect. A great soul will be strong to live as well as think though," said Ralph Waldo Emerson. Your soul is made to act on your dreams. The best education leads us to listen with our hearts. Do it now with confidence in yourself.

"Learning doesn't have a destination, neither does the imagination,"

– Arthur J. Rutledge.

A is for Attitude

I often say, "The attitude with which we make our decisions can predict our conditions in life." I remember the wise words of Zig Ziglar, who said, "It's not your aptitude but your attitude that determines your altitude," in that compelling way he presented it! He truly understood the power of attitude.

He knew how to convey his message with as much energy as a wild bronco. His communication was crystal clear, partly due to knowing how to elevate his energy beyond the physical. Attitude is precisely that—being able to rise above it all. This is a spiritual understanding and requires a mastery of oneself. It represents the highest form of consciousness, and individuals with this type of vibration resonate deeply with others. Their words hold power and are in harmonious sync with their intention of giving love. I say this because you possess that power too. It only requires a decision to believe in your unique ability to give unconditionally.

I believe the best start in any endeavor is being intentional with a positive attitude. It will bolster the actions that speak volumes and triumph over the whispers of fear. Our dreams emanate from the master of the universe. You are meant to discover your purpose, and it's aligned with your dream in some way. It took me 30 years to start fulfilling my purpose. Stay the course. Trust in the flow as you grow. Build confidence and bring an attitude of joy on your journey.

M is for Motivation

I had the privilege of becoming certified as part of the John Maxwell Team (JMT) Leadership 2020. It was a significant steppingstone for me, driven by my motivation to join his organization long before that. Four years prior, I had embarked on a journey of self-development with the best MLM organization and was introduced to Dr. John C. Maxwell's mindset through Success magazine.

In 2014, I received 'Success Magazine' CDs as part of my subscription, which I eagerly consumed to cultivate my mindset and grow my business. Enthusiasm fluctuated over the years, experiencing highs and lows. By the first and third year, I had become a leader with considerable momentum.

Darren Hardy's Compound Effect was working in my favor, shaping my confidence and my dream.

Seeing John C. Maxwell in person at our international convention was just the beginning. The next step was buying and reading his outstanding book, "Sometimes You Win, Sometimes You Learn," and continuing to invest in consuming the right knowledge while applying it.

I had to learn all the components necessary for dreams to materialize, as mentioned above. I was fortunate to be the right person at the right time to accept what was being taught. Dr. John C. Maxwell would often ask, "Are we being teachable?" I now understand more than I ever thought possible after these 10 years.

I learned three significant lessons about motivation:

First, motivation doesn't happen on demand; your dream will grow in proportion to the effort you put into it daily.

Second, motivation is fleeting, so you must have a big enough "why" to keep you grounded until your emotional state transitions into a disciplined one.

Third, I learned to be patient while remaining productive as I marched from where I was toward the person I was becoming. Motivation is the energy that springs forth between sweat, tears, discomfort, and disappointment on the way to your victories.

Confidence is the strengthening of character that arises from persistence. If you desire your dreams to come true, it all comes down to how hard you are willing to work to achieve them. Finally, in John C. Maxwell's "15 Invaluable Laws of Growth," he discusses the law of consistency. Motivation gets you going, but discipline ensures you keep growing. Believe that!

While everybody may have a dream, not many are willing to work hard for something intangible. For most, if it's untouchable, it's inconceivable. The real path to achievement lies in conceiving it, believing in it, and then receiving it. As the Good Book says, anyone who will have everlasting life must believe in receiving it.

It may seem like pie in the sky for some and unimaginable for others but imagine your dreams with a ladder in your hands and a fork in your pocket! Confidence makes that pie even sweeter!

The Law of Obsolescence dictates that everything—products, services, skills, core competencies, advertisements, marketing strategies, and business processes—is gradually becoming obsolete with the passing of time.

Here are some insights from Brian Tracy from his book "100 Laws of Business Success":

Laws of Obsolescence:

1. Tomorrow will be different than today.
2. Continuing innovation and improvement are essential to survival.
3. The best way to predict the future is to create it.

Keep your dream fresh and stay optimistic about what it will become over time.

"Learning doesn't have a destination, neither does the imagination."

– Arthur J. Rutledge

Stay away from being a worry wart!

Ralph Waldo Emerson said, "As a cure for worrying, work is better than whiskey." Don't abuse yourself or your dreams by doing erosive activities that disintegrate good intentions. Always hold in your heart at every moment that you will make this time different. Hope with action makes the dreams real. nothing else will make you do until you know persistence is up to you, my friend. Here are 4 steps to stop worrying: from the author of "How to Make Friends and Influence People" gives to change your Woo's to weapons of confidence titled: "How to Stop Worrying & Start Living."

- Writing down precisely what I'm worried about.
- Writing down what I can do about it.
- Deciding what to do.
- Start immediate action to carry out that decision.

Intentional Awareness is to know what works in our favor and doesn't work.

Gary Keller & Jay Papasan in, "The One Thing" says "The 4 thieves for productivity" are:

- The inability to say no
- The fear of chaos
- Poor health habits
- Remaining in an environment that doesn't support your goals

Poem

Our imagination gives our
experiences with new interpretations and
is a key in the rejuvenation of purpose.
This Fresh air of intention points
the way to see and seize vast opportunities.
Imagination gives insight necessary for
our mind to open untapped possibilities.

Being creatively agile in our conditioning can make us stronger in every aspect of life and our self-potential be promulgated to the world.

Jóhann Jóhannsson puts it simply by stating, "Find the thing you do well and do it again and again for the rest of your life."

Feelings & Thoughts

____

____

____

____

____

____

____

____

____

____

____

____

____

CHAPTER THREE

Let go to Grow

*If you can't do great things,
do small things in a great way.*

– Napoleon Hill

*By developing a mindset that says everything is
coming, you develop an energy that says keep going.*

– Norman Gordon "The Poetry Man."

Don't just plan based on the past; it will put you in last place. Keep your faith in the fact that you never stop growing from where you were before.

*Always stay present with who you are from
moment to moment & period to period.*

– Arthur Rutledge

In my life I have let go of many ideas, people, places, possessions, prideful things.

Pridefulness can be the enemy of good. Here are some let goes that you have probably let go or still holding to:

- We let go to make room for new growth.
- We let go to take on bigger and better things in our lives.
- We let go of the cynical thinking for the optimistic scenario.
- We let go of a set mind on little for a vast constructive mindset.
- We let go of chaos for serenity.
- We let go of scarcity for abundance.
- We let go of fakeness for our authenticity.

The things we haven't let go of for our own good could come back to haunt us. At worst, they could create unforeseen delays or distractions in our future. These challenges serve as the ultimate test for us.

So, ask yourself: Do you truly want what's best for yourself?

If the answer is yes, then be prepared to make difficult decisions. Strengthen your confidence by practicing habits like delayed gratification and letting go of what you can't control. My friend and author, Dr. Karim R. Ellis, emphasizes, "Faith that can't be tested can't be trusted."

I couldn't agree more; if it's not tested, it's not true. We demonstrate our faith in ourselves by bringing our actions to our attention. Your confidence will grow and become more focused as you let go of things that don't support efficient living.

The work of being productive often begins with something as simple as cleaning out closets.

I was terrible at chores growing up. My mother never stopped telling me, "I don't want you to be a man that can't take care of his responsibilities. Everything is a prerequisite to maturity. Just because the task seems small, don't get used to overlooking things. I won't always be here to clean up your messes." I partially understood what she was saying. I can't tell you whether it was that I didn't know or didn't care. Probably both. I soon found out that what you don't do now will affect you sooner or later.

I don't know why I thought having a job was a good idea; I couldn't even do tasks around the house where I slept and ate. Nevertheless, I was super excited to be the first kid I knew to get a job at 12 years old at Burger King.

The local Detroit multi-millionaire entrepreneur, Brady Keys, opened a chain of these franchises over the metro area. The program I was working in allowed children a chance (with parents' permission, of course) to participate with pay on a part-time basis. Weekends only, so as not to interfere with the children's curriculum.

I found out quickly what we all find out eventually about work: they pay you because it's laborious, not because it's fun.

My friends were in disbelief that I would work and didn't have to. To be honest, I liked working more than I thought I would. Yes, the kid who constantly dismissed his chores did okay on his first job. It gave me a feeling of self-respect and something bigger on some level.

What did I have to give up, you may ask? A bit of my adolescence for a future look of maturity. A touch of my excuses for a trip into self-discipline. A lot of inadequacies for a beginner's guide to confidence. I did so well with the good habits I picked up, working into the summer and the rest of that year. Going from maintenance tasks to the broiler to the board. The board was where they made the orders. I was super-fast. I also got along with the staff.

The checks were super low, but the satisfaction of making my own money was priceless. I don't know whether I outgrew my job or whether their program ended. I also know that that wasn't a career choice for me. I wouldn't have known that if I hadn't taken a job.

That's a valuable lesson in itself: discovering what doesn't click for you sooner rather than later. Remember, we are all in a race against time. That's why acting is a better teacher than overthinking.

Too much analysis leads to anxiety, but action beats paralysis. It's only when you let your mind know how courageous your heart is that you can truly progress!

During that chapter of my life, my mom allowed me to come to conclusions for myself, of course, with both strong and gentle nudges along my teenage journey.

It's a pivotal point in our lives when we get to decide whether to keep going or simply keep moving. These shifts will define who you grow into based on how much you're willing to accept yourself.

We all understand what that was like in 2020, the year the earth seemed to stand still. Pivots and reconstructions of our existence were taken to another level. Most of us found a way forward from unimaginable circumstances. Did you do it? Are you still working it out? The answer is probably yes.

The good news is that you're still standing and moving forward. Congratulations on your continued comeback. Courage is just that: continuing to come back. That's also what inspires your commitment to self-confidence.

I mentioned delayed gratification earlier. It's associated with resisting a smaller but more immediate reward in order to receive a larger or more enduring reward later.

A growing body of literature has linked the ability to delay gratification to a host of other positive outcomes, including academic success, physical health, psychological health, and social competence. Letting go of expectations or overemotional use is a good practice to clear the mind. It provides clarity to what you truly want to accomplish in any aspect of your life.

These levels of inner or intrinsic control can keep us in touch with our purest potential. I've faced many trials in life, and most were me putting my own self on trial for little things that seemed bigger at the time. It slowed me down from achieving what I desired. Activity on things that are not productive unless you are crystal clear on what you want and why you want it.

These units of understanding are glimpses into your self-control. Accepting who you really are will make you feel uncomfortable and uncertain more times than not. What does it say about anyone who can't move that rubber tree plant? That ant stayed in high hopes! Not low hopes or desperation, but high hopes. High trust. High faith. High confidence. Nobody can take it away from you without your permission.

Giving up some things helps you better serve other things. Pick up level headedness, assertiveness, self-reliance, self-respect, and the optimism of an open mind. There's so much more productivity in a creative mind. Put down insecurity, indifference, timidity, uncertainty, and pessimism. These don't serve your cause and stop you from being at cause.

Facing and being accountable for your thoughts and actions is being at fault for yourself. That's the only empathic empowerment you need to face any lapse of self-confidence. Clearing your mind with confidence will liberate you.

As I mentioned earlier that first job served as a catalyst for my awareness. I was years ahead of my peers and worked out ways to make strong decisions. Becoming more sure of myself motivated me to seek out more work, even if I wasn't sure what kind of work I would enjoy. It equipped me with the right mindset to handle whatever came my way. Furthermore, I learned to detach myself from unnecessary emotional states of stress. This transformation allowed me to become the authentic, laid-back person you're chatting with now.

There is a universal law called "The Law of Detachment." It is a spiritual practice centered around letting go of worry and allowing things to happen. It can be summarized by the mantra, "Release and let go." I personally use mantras like "let go, let God" and "faith it till you make it" to put myself in the right state of attitude and energy. To apply the Law of Detachment, it's essential to let go of what's no longer serving you and open your mind to all possibilities.

4 facts to keep you thriving in this confidence tug-a-war:

1. Confidence is an attribute that will help you to perform under pressure.
2. Confidence contributes to being decisive in whatever you set your heart on.
3. Confront your confidence by doing the things that you may not like or what to do even if for only a short period because getting out of your comfort zone will also put you in the top 80% of people who are in won't land.

4. Confidence is the condition that gets you out of the dugout and onto the field. Win, lose, or draw it reminds you that you're stronger for the experience.

"Become competent in the little things repeatedly and over time you become boundless in everything!"

– Arthur j. Rutledge

You truly succeed in life when you know and walk in your worth become one. Value your value!

We can't become truly resilient if we don't learn to navigate through pain. Pain serves as a crucial teacher in our journey. It's essential to develop techniques that help you confront and manage your emotions, allowing you to cultivate resilience and a stronger state of mind.

Empowerment comes from acknowledging that you have the capacity to handle whatever life throws your way, evening the playing field and feeling competent in your ability to overcome challenges.

Feelings & Thoughts

CHAPTER FOUR

Keep Your Eyes on the Target

"I'm enjoying every moment of it, with every event my confidence to achieve my target is increasing."

– Samresh Jung

Personal or professional goals find higher levels with committed focus to your purpose. Persistence in focus turns our dreams into reality. And, without mental or emotional focus, we'll fall short of getting any dream worth having.

From childhood to adulthood, there are many things that can slow us down and often cause us to take our eyes off of life's proverbial ball. Anything and everything we want to accomplish needs nutrition.

The principle of living our best life is in the daily steps we take to see, know and act towards our goals. Embracing challenges can also be difficult when there aren't a lot of options available to get educated with elementary tools given by society. Tools that enable us to develop certain skills that can be useful to raise personal competency.

When these times come, and they will. It's always good practice to itemize ten or more of your strengths and talents in order to keep focused on believing in you. You may have heard this phrase before: "Only what you focus on expands."

Believing in what you're aiming to achieve matters. No matter what season you're in, the acknowledgment of these ten strengths can open your mind to a better you and will make your target easier to hit.

What options are available to you for becoming the success you desire? Even if there aren't ten strengths that you can think of right now, start directing your attention to them over the next week. Focusing on tasks like this will increase self-awareness & self-confidence.

As the saying goes, "The little things mean a lot". This only applies if you can keep yourself focused on the single target with your strongest talent.

Five steps to F.O.C.U.S

1. Follow what you committed to do
2. One project or task at a time
3. Course is consistent work to progress in your season

4. Until success, daily sharpening skills, learning and evaluation.
5. Success is to be expected only through the focus of your heart's desire

"Talent hits the target that no one else can hit. Genius hits the target no one else can see."

– Arthur Schopenhauer

And, as Paulo Coelho quipped," No one can hit the target with their eyes closed!"

Focusing on who you are identifies where you are and helps you to stay open to who you are becoming. This is how you can decide where you want to go. Your confidence will assist in accomplishing anything you want while cultivating self-respect that's built through daily soul searching and an exercising of the mind.

During my adolescent years, there were many things I enjoyed doing; singing in a few groups, singing in the choir, dancing, basketball, roller skating, video games & hosting gatherings in my backyard garage, to name a few.

As I reflect on those days, I realize all the support I received from my family & friends. Even if a person does exactly what they desire, not many people like to take that ride alone. Our mentors & coaches are the unsung heroes who hold us up while rooting for us as we get lifelong wins.

You might say "I've never needed anyone but me to do the things I needed to get done". While your recollection may have some truth, we must acknowledge that a child doesn't learn to stand, walk, or learn a new skill without an encouraging person or environment. Encouragement comes through those who support your experience.

Trust is taught and during the process it is learned.

The things I did gave me joy. And, in doing what gave me the most joy, I felt that I was succeeding in those talents.

My self-trust grew with the things I was consistently good at doing. Which put certain beliefs into clear view. The power of confidence comes first from acknowledging who you are & then feeling fulfilled in what you do feels authentic enough to complement your inner person.

The philosopher and theologian Rumi asserted: "Respond to every call that excites your spirit." When something comes from your heart, it will always call to you. Persistently focusing on those important things can support the uplifting of our spirits. We've heard the saying "trust the process". Well, your eyes must first develop the skill of discipline to focus on your target.

With that, there really is no target until focus is patiently acquired. Focus is as essential to a process as fruit is to a tree. Trust is the persistence of a person's truth and creating a process. Your focus shows your mind why it creates its truth.

"Productivity is never an accident. It is always the result of a commitment to excellence, intelligent planning and focused effort.

– "Paul J. Meyer

Anything around you can disrupt your focus until we practice these 3 things:

1. Accepting the fact
2. Accepting silencing our mind
3. Accepting our mistakes

Stay committed to focus & your focus will hit the target of any goal you can imagine.

Feelings & Thoughts

CHAPTER FIVE

Being Present is Fulfillment

You have the opportunity to be present, to discern your purpose, and to commit to the necessary work to achieve it. On the other hand, to be your best self, it's essential to understand fulfillment. It involves curiosity about your past and present experiences, ensuring alignment with who you are destined to become.

So, the pivotal question arises: Are you fulfilled? Are you in the job you desire? What changes have you made from last year to this year, or every year, that contribute to your sense of fulfillment? How much attention do you devote to nurturing the best version of yourself? Satisfaction in life doesn't come from just one aspect: it's a multifaceted pursuit. Embrace patience and love as you navigate life's complexities. Solutions to challenges eventually emerge through self-discipline.

I recently came across a quote by Steven Maraboli: "Forget yesterday, it has already forgotten you. Don't sweat tomorrow, you haven't met it yet. Open your eyes and your heart to a truly precious today."

I resonate with the essence of living in the moment and looking towards the future. However, I believe that ignoring yesterday doesn't propel us forward. The past serves as a source of reflection and inspiration. Forgiveness for past mistakes is essential for a healthy present. Reflecting with awareness and gratitude allows us to accept the past as a lesson, not a burden.

We mustn't allow ourselves to be held captive by past fears. Stagnation in the past breeds a lack of confidence and hopelessness. Finding fulfillment in life requires hope.

As a spring cannot pour out both sweet and bitter water from the same opening, the mind cannot forget until it forgives. The journey from reflection to awareness is a process; avoid projecting old hurts onto others. Discipline is required in navigating all aspects of the past.

To overcome the challenges of the present, one must confront and overcome their past fears. Achieving fulfillment and discovering one's purpose requires this courageous confrontation. Mastery over this process leads to a fuller life and a profound understanding of one's own power, enabling confident pursuit of any purpose one is drawn to.

As author and poet James Allen beautifully expressed, "To confront aimlessness and weakness, and to begin to think with purpose, is to enter the ranks of those strong ones who only recognize failure as one of the pathways to attainment, who make all conditions serve them, and who think strongly, attempt fearlessly, and accomplish masterfully."

Aimlessness arises from uncertainties and insecurities, weakening us when we feel choked off from our potential and lack the hope to navigate through. This downward mindset corrodes the very essence of our strength.

If aimlessness and weakness resonate with your experience, it's essential to address past pains that undermine your anticipated confidence. Vision requires trust in us, leading to the fulfillment of purpose and belief in favorable outcomes.

Renowned motivational speaker and author Les Brown, aptly states, "Too many of us are not living our dreams because we are living our fears." I always emphasize that facing our fears is the path to personal growth and enlightenment. Clarity lightens our burden, bringing peace of mind and highlighting our present purpose while relegating past pain to its rightful place in our journey.

We acknowledge its lessons and forgive ourselves, allowing us to move forward with faith and self-belief, akin to the rhythmic precision of a grandfather clock, or the majestic presence of Big Ben in London. Bold and beautiful, we lay down our past and embrace clarity, refusing to linger in darkness.

Helen Keller wisely advised, "Keep your face to the sunshine and you cannot see a shadow." Let go of shadows to find fulfillment, recognizing them as transient projections of our fears.

It's our choice whether to dwell in self-made despair or bask in the abundance of the sun. This book serves as an opportunity to reinvent and recommit to living with a vertical mindset, rejecting indecision and embracing action.

As you read these words, I implore you to make the call to action, to enrich your life with experiences that bring significance and live intentionally, inspired to make every moment count.

> ***"The most difficult thing is the decision to act, the rest is merely tenacity."***
>
> ***– Amelia Earhart***

Self-belief is a daily practice that must be cultivated consistently. Success in any endeavor requires attentiveness to our actions and decisions. Building unwavering confidence necessitates inner faith and a deep-seated belief that our choices serve our future outcomes. Regardless of our current circumstances, we are always just one decision away from reaffirming our commitment to our vision.

Edward Bulwer-Lytton eloquently expresses this concept: "The people who excel in life clearly discern their objective and habitually direct their powers towards that object. Even genius itself is but fine observation strengthened by fixity of purpose. Every person who observes vigilantly and resolves steadfastly grows into a genius."

For further exploration of purpose and vision, I highly recommend two books: "Find Your Why" by Simon Sinek and "Put Your Dream to the Test" by John C. Maxwell. These resources offer valuable insights and guidance to help you clarify your objectives and pursue them with unwavering determination.

Following through on your desires with excellence fosters self-trust and self-efficacy.

While some resilience is inherent in our human nature, the rest is a conscious decision to persevere until we realize our true strength.

Remember the words of Rumi: "You are not a drop in the ocean; you are the mighty ocean in the drop." Though you may feel small at times, you possess the potential to unleash a tidal wave of impact if you dare to believe in yourself!

Now, with that empowering reminder, let me offer you some actionable steps to enhance your confidence and foster your growth:

1. Organize a good Sleep regiment
2. Be on the lookout for new opportunities
3. Respect others
4. Meditate
5. Exercise regularly and seek a nutritionist
6. Read plan/constructive learning
7. Get a mindset coach

8. Set goals/ Plan ahead
9. Stay optimistic to realize your purpose (If don't know already)
10. Inspire others
11. Learn from failures
12. Help others
13. Track progress
14. Journal
15. Keep learning
16. Build relationships/Network
17. Delegate your time
18. Learn new skills/Stay productive
19. Delegate your time
20. Bring joy to your journey
21. Be kind to yourself with every effort

Poem

"Resilience is silent and deep, like roots.
It doesn't announce itself.
It doesn't explode outward.
It doesn't fall.
It doesn't break.
It simply always is.
And you are."
Victoria Erickson, Author, Edge of Wonder

Some splendid songs serve to remind me of my power. Music just has that power, doesn't it? From close friend Terry Dexter's "Beautiful One" to Des'ree's "You Gotta Be", I like to suggest getting and listening to the words.

Pick a song that touches you to the heart, even to tears. Tears break down and unclog us to a deep level of devotion. You can be free to love yourself as God intended you to be. When you devote your time to this over time, you will be cleansed from the shortsightedness of you.

Each day will start with your face to the sky and soul to the sun. While listening to songs about or the ones of your choosing, put your hand over your heart and with a smile on your face. Do this daily for 33 days.

Breathe in the empowering words! Throw in closing your eyes. When closing off one part of the five senses, the others get more energized. Heart, mind, and gut get to have all that's yummy self-love! Hm, hm, feel the love, self-value abounds! That's the type of feeling you get to have on this path to the right communication to yourself.

You have a resilient spirit. You are the unique creation of the master of the universe. Show yourself what you are made of my friend. Feelings of fulfillment, wholeheartedness, unflinching, and stalwart integrity are grown from the inside out, not the outside in. Confidence is the fulfillment that fortifies and allows you the freedom to accept your future successes!

Feelings & Thoughts

CHAPTER SIX

Connect, Consider, and Convert

"Discipline is choosing between what you want now and what you want most"

~ Abraham Lincoln

"Don't be pushed around by the fears in your mind. Be led by the dreams in your heart."

~ Roy T. Bennet

"Imagine breaking through the barrier of self-doubt and becoming the person YOU were BORN TO BE!"

~ Jamie Kern Lima

When I was younger, I took a lot of things for granted.

I thought I would figure out the direction of my life sooner rather than later. However, it turned out to be later than sooner. It wasn't because I didn't mean well or lacked ideas; it was due to a lack of knowledge and confidence. Often in life, we make it hard on ourselves by searching for a window to climb out of instead of simply using the door. We are meant to walk through the door.

No matter how crusty, chipped, corroded, or unpleasant it may seem, it leads us to the next steps of our journey, even if we don't have a clue what those steps might be. All you need is acceptance of whatever lies beyond that door.

Facing reality is tough, but it's also liberating. Feel free to experience whatever emotions arise as you walk through these "doors of life." Clarity about who you are is constantly evolving from moment to moment; that's what I call your "event horizon."

James Allen expressed a similar sentiment, stating, "There is no comforter to compare with goodwill for dispersing the shadows of grief and sorrow. To live continually in thoughts of ill will, cynicism, suspicion, and envy is to be confined in a self-made prison-hole.

But to think well of all, to be cheerful with all, to patiently learn to find the good in all—such unselfish thoughts are the very portals of heaven; and to dwell day by day in thoughts of peace toward every creature will bring abounding peace to their possessor."

The repeated trust that you give yourself will gain momentum as you go through your daily routine and consciously tackle tasks, goals, and deadlines. I, too, didn't have it all figured out. I remember feeling restless and preoccupied with discovering my purpose. I was trying too hard to mold myself into someone I wanted to become, and I found that it was breaking me.

I began searching for reliable guidance to help me find answers about who I wanted to be and immediate solutions on how I could get there. Besides my mother and grandmother, there weren't many people I looked up to as authoritative figures and wasn't intimidated by. However, I had one person I could talk to because he always told me his door was open for me: Dr. Reverend Odell Jones, the spiritual leader of my church, Pleasant Grove Baptist Church.

Dr. Jones was well-known in the Baptist community in Detroit and nationally. It seemed like we had a different guest speaker at our church every other week. Me and a few others looked up to him like a godfather. I thought of him as the wisest man in any conversation, and perhaps overqualified for what I considered to be my minor concerns.

Nevertheless, I knew I needed help, and who better than him?

Don't get me wrong, mom and grandma were great to confide in, but when someone is a regular fixture in your life, for some reason, we tend to discount what they have to say. I'm sure you can relate on some level! I wanted to hear a different perspective, especially a male version of life. Strong male figures were less common than their female counterparts at that time, and probably even less so nowadays. Moreover, Dr. Jones was the closest person I considered successful in life.

I set up an appointment with the church secretary, Ms. Marsh, as per his request. It felt strange talking to him in his office or in the passing, but I felt a bit nervous when I made it all formal. I must have been 15 or 16 at the time. I walked into his office and my gaze wandered to the walls adorned with pictures of presidents and church dignitaries, then down slowly to him, wearing an accomplished warm smile. It was a usual pattern every time I was in his office.

He asked if I was going to sing another solo in choir and how I was doing with the church basketball team to kick off the conversation. Most of the time, I excitedly replied with a "yes, soon" or "very good." I then adopted a more serious demeanor and asked him what it was like to be popular.

He exuded confidence and inspired his congregation with a sense of being that they all seemed to celebrate. After posing my question, he paused and gazed deeply at me, so intensely it felt like he could see into my soul. Rev was truly a force of God, and I sensed that something profound was about to be revealed.

He said, "You are popular, and you are also a leader." He continued, "I see a light in you and in all the children of the church. You listen to your mother, you're actively involved in 4 auxiliaries, you help your friends, and you are always pleasant, as a child of God should be. I have been blessed by God to have a congregation that does good work in His name.

Whatever you may think of yourself, know that all you need is God, and He will provide everything you need in His own time. Trust in Him. I trust that you will persist in doing good."

After he finished speaking, he stood and enveloped me in a warm bear hug. Much later in my life, I realized through the effort and effectiveness of leadership that leaders find and refine ways to enable others to shine! He then asked, "Was there anything else?"...I replied, "Yes. Can I come back again?"...His answer was, "Anytime."

I wasn't much of a conversationalist at that moment, but what he said and the way he said it gave me an unexpected moment of clarity. Rev instilled within me a sense of accomplishment. Through the act of listening and from that listening, I discovered my being.

I understood that if I continued doing the right things and being good, I could find more satisfaction and success in whatever I decided for myself. As I implemented that advice in my life, I also remained in a state of constant curiosity. I began asking better questions and learning things that connected me to a deeper sense of fulfillment in life, and even better... how to live it to the fullest.

It took someone who saw something in me that I didn't see in myself to reveal my significance. I have been progressively pursuing the things I want for myself, without much concern for those who could potentially slow me down. As my esteemed pastor so lovingly instilled confidence in me, he said I have a light in me and encouraged me to trust in God. Both a godfather figure and a father in God believe in me. Even when it doesn't feel like it at times, I believe it's always the Father above who believes in you.

Preparing yourself is the prerogative of any person to shift the pendulum in your favor. Having courage in what you're pursuing will tip the scales of inadequacy toward a transition of self-assurance. Years later, while living and working in Milan, Italy, Reverend Jones passed away. I was devastated that I couldn't say a last farewell to him. However, even though he passed from this plane, his brave words never fell to the ground. Like all great leaders, he was able to pass on his insight and wisdom to me through many conversations sparked by my initiative for growth.

He, along with several other mentors I encountered over the years who lived confidently in their own zones, enabled me to make my life fuller. Twelve countries later, as an international top model with friends all over the world, none of this would have come to pass in the spectacular way it did without their guidance. I recall a Chinese proverb that says, "To know the road ahead, ask those coming back." Reverend Jones and others like him provided sage perspectives that expanded my vision of myself. Thanks to them, I was able to enhance my experiences and embrace new ways of living far beyond what I could have imagined as a traveler from Detroit.

The great and beloved wizard of the Harry Potter stories, Professor Albus Dumbledore, famously imbued, "Help will always be given to those who ask for it!"

Being open to trusting someone takes time or, more often than not, breaking free from the mundaneness that you're accustomed to feeling. Meeting the right people can exorcise your comfort zone without the fear of experiencing a spinning head like in the movies. Pain only hurts for a time, and you grow stronger in that area of life.

Throughout my life, I have unintentionally stepped on some toes. To those affected, I offer my sincere apologies! It takes enduring grit to rise to your best form. Grit is the friction required to attain self-freedom, to be self-conscious of every level of your potential.

I honed my confidence by observing people who approached life the way I aspired to. I also learned valuable lessons from those who didn't want me to progress further or achieve more. It's essential to recognize that even those who appear to be on the rise have faced setbacks. Therefore, be cautious of whose advice you heed, and always approach it with as much confidence as you can muster. You don't want to put yourself at a disadvantage when striving to be confident. There's no imposter when you're improving yourself through discipline.

There's nothing to conceal when your disciplines are firmly established. Opportunities become commonplace when you allow your mind to operate with open anticipation. Whatever good you aim to achieve, persist in it, and you will witness your possibilities expanding.

John C. Maxwell provides a compelling analogy in the chapter on the law of timing in his book "The 21 Irrefutable Laws of Leadership." He compares leadership to baseball, highlighting the critical role of timing. The difference between hitting a home run and a foul ball often comes down to timing. When the ball is thrown, if the batter swings too slowly, they miss the connection.

On the other hand, swinging too quickly also results in a missed opportunity. The key in life, Maxwell suggests, is to keep swinging—persisting, practicing, evaluating, and maintaining self-belief. Become confident in what you can control and find comfort in what's beyond your control.

Have faith in your endeavors and trust that they will bear fruit in due time. Don't walk away from the plate until you're skilled enough to know you can hit the ball. Stand firm, adopt the correct position and stance, keep your eyes focused, and let your prepared efforts guide you toward success. Maxwell's advice is clear: keep swinging until you get it right. I like to call that "Shine time!"

"You truly succeed in life when the actions of knowing your worth and walking in your worth become one. Value your value."

– Arthur J Rutledge"

Be the person who understands that getting knocked down is a necessary part of the journey. Recognize that with error comes understanding, and through calamity, whispers of competency emerge. Struggles shock the system into creative sustainability and foster growth in self-trust.

Your true competitor is not found in front of you or beside you, but within you. This truth becomes evident only through the work that is required and calls upon every individual.

Keep these three steps in mind as you're getting good at or mastering vertical confidence:

1. Maintain a Beginner's Mindset with Patience:

   Approach your journey with a beginner's mindset and patience. This attitude will help you remain open to learning and growth, allowing you to see the opportunities that are meant for you. Understand that not everything in life is meant for you, regardless of your level of confidence. Let go of things that don't serve you and focus on what truly matters.

2. Embrace Challenges and Growth:

   Cultivate a bigger-than-life attitude every day. Seek out or create new challenges that push you outside of your comfort zone. Understand that anything worth having is often more challenging at the beginning than at the end. Embrace the journey of building confidence, knowing that there is no limit to where it can take you.

3. Engage in Inner and Outer Action:

    Inner strength and trust grow stronger through inner action and interaction. Embrace the zest you may have been missing for months, years, or even decades. Get active by joining groups, teams, communities, or cultural activities, and don't make excuses for not knowing where to start. Reach out to current friends or colleagues for guidance and support. Make it a priority and commit to the most important goal: knowing the self-love within you and sharing that trust with others.

As Marcus Aurelius wisely said, "If you are distressed by anything, the pain is not due to the thing itself but to your own estimate of it; and this you have the power to revoke at any moment." Overthinking and being unnerved by things beyond our control doesn't lead to better results. It takes the same confidence to live a lonely life as it does to connect with others. Confidence empowers us to take control over our emotions and live our fullest lives.

Look to the sky and realize that all the stars together create the most wonderful displays of grandeur. We shine the brightest when we come together as one. Own and cherish your value in the world. I'm reminded of James Allen's quote: "Make all conditions serve you.

Think strongly, attempt fearlessly, and accomplish mastery." Show your commitment to yourself by daring to attempt and pursue mastery. Growth awaits those who persist, and we only grow from what we know.

In the words of Diana Ross's famous song, "Reach out and touch somebody's hand, make this world a better place if we can." Let us all strive to make a positive impact by connecting with and supporting one another on our journeys.

Visualize yourself surrounded by others who can lean into your confidence, sharing smiles, hugs, handshakes, and transformative ideas that have shaped mankind for eternity. These authentic interactions inspire compassion and drive interconnected and interdependent change in the world. Together, we can make a positive impact by supporting and uplifting one another, fostering a sense of unity and collective purpose.

> "Accept the things to which fate binds you and love the people with whom fate brings you together but do so with all your heart".
>
> *– Marcus Aurelius*

God believed in us first, and the reverend allowed me to catch his light. Through this book, I am determined to show you my belief in you as I pass you a torch, allowing you to see your unquestionable value and live anew. Shine on!

Feelings & Thoughts

CHAPTER SEVEN

'I Am' the Mantra

*"There is something you must always remember.
You are braver than you believe, stronger than you
seem, and smarter than you think."*

– A.A. Milne

Self-belief, the signature of one's greatness, unveils a person's truth to the world: 'I am here!' This lesson was one I had to learn repeatedly while growing up in my neighborhood, navigating various jobs, and attending social gatherings.

Building self-belief can be challenging, particularly while seeking acceptance. I overcame the hurdle of people-pleasing during high school, where my fashion sense, amiable yet not arrogant demeanor, and extracurricular activities were mostly outside of school.

I discovered that genuine connections were forged by those willing to be authentic rather than those claiming authority. By sticking to the things I enjoyed until I was satisfied or ready to pivot to something new, I established my self-worth. At that time, my passions included dancing, basketball, and exploring new places.

From 11th grade until seven years later, I experienced extensive travel with my Detroit companions, Aton and Charles. Aton, my schoolmate from John J. Pershing Doughboys, and Charles, a friend from Pleasant Grove Baptist Church, were my most reliable companions. Together, we embarked on trips to Toledo, Cleveland, Chicago, D.C., Virginia, and even weathered a tornado.

Aton, besides being my first entrepreneurial friend among my peers, was the one I relied on the most. Our adventures ranged from choir rehearsals to visiting various churches on Sundays, driving to both familiar and unknown destinations, playing basketball, and enjoying video games.

It was an extraordinary time in my life to have friends like them and several others who instilled in me the 'courage called confidence' in the person I was becoming. I dared to be myself because I was surrounded by people who also dared to be, despite uncertainty. Through them, I learned about their talents, gifts, and strengths, which allowed me to reflect on my own, even acknowledging my weaknesses and areas of rigidity. This self-awareness was invaluable in understanding who I am and what I am capable of.

Author and motivational teacher Jim Rohn imparts wisdom, advising, 'Get around people who have something of value to share with you. Their impact will continue to have a significant effect on your life long after they have departed.' A good friendship possesses the power to uplift and inspire.

I suggest nurturing your confidence through positive interactions with people who uplift you, engaging in activities that resonate with your heart, and pursuing work that ignites your passion. Author Marianne Williamson echoes this sentiment, stating, "King Solomon, who supposedly was the wisest of all people, described his youth as his winter and his advanced years as his summer.

We can be older than we used to be yet feel much younger than we are." If your confidence seems out of season, be patient and love yourself. As long as you remain intentional about building it through stepping out of your comfort zone, you will eventually find your stride. Even if you haven't been fortunate enough to have confidants like mine, investing in your confidence will prove to yourself that you can.

Types of qualities people should have for smooth interaction or communication:

- Emotional Intelligence
- Mood Mastery
- Self-Awareness
- Emotional Wellness
- Empathy and Connection

- Personal Growth
- Mindfulness
- Resilience Building
- Emotional Health Education
- Supportive Community
- Inner Peace
- Transformative Emotional Journeys
- Healing through Understanding
- Emotion-Focused Storytelling
- Nurturing Emotional Fitness
- Insightful Reflections
- Empowering Emotions
- Holistic Development

Roman statesman and Stoic philosopher Seneca once said, "Associate with people who are likely to improve you. Welcome those whom you are capable of improving. The process is mutual; people learn as they teach." It's a dynamic dance that keeps us on our toes, reminding us of who we are not as we navigate these interactions of self-discovery.

When you consciously introduce yourself to yourself, reshaping your character to attain the confidence you seek, it may be easier at times than others to identify these types of individuals.

Nevertheless, it's a process well worth undertaking. The more confidently you show up, the better equipped you become to manage the lows and highs of emotional well-being. Practice makes perfect in every aspect of life.

It's essential to acknowledge that as you embark on this journey of self-realization, there are no shortcuts to feeling complete.

While the path may seem straightforward in theory, the reality of piecing it all together can be messy. Maintain your commitment to becoming a stronger, more self-sufficient version of yourself, embracing both the good and the challenging aspects that ultimately shape our wholeness.

Forget perfection; embrace the imperfections that lead to triumph. Make the choice to persist until you achieve your goals, staying true to yourself along the way. Success is earned through hard work and dedication. Accomplishment in life comes from becoming proficient in the knowledge of what it takes to elevate from ordinary to extraordinary. True confidence is about being willing to endure challenges to reach greater heights. Chaka Khan's song "Through the Fire" encapsulates this sentiment in its chorus: "Through the fire, to the limit, to the wall, for a chance to be with you, I'd gladly risk it all."

These passionate words speak to an engagement with another, but I understand that such a connection begins with oneself. It involves making a declaration to the person who needs it most—yourself.

Take the time to feel what's needed while asking yourself, 'Who am I?' Reflect on what brings you joy and fulfillment. When do you feel your best? Who are your truest confidants? How can you learn to trust yourself?

What are your next steps in life? These questions, and more, can only find their answers through unwavering commitment—"through the fire, to the limit, to the wall, and risking it all." Outer results stem from inner commitments.

Commitment is the 'I AM' that communicates your truth. It serves as proof to yourself that you are capable and confident enough to pursue your desires.

True confidence arises from an awareness that certain experiences can hurt us, change us, and ultimately transform us.

As Virginia Woolf once said, "I will go on adventuring, changing, opening my mind and my eyes, refusing to be stamped and stereotyped. The thing is to free oneself: to let it find its dimensions, not be impeded."

The best way to begin any endeavor is with intentionality and the correct attitude. This mindset supports actions that speak volumes and triumph over the whispers of fear.

Promises are commitments made with integrity, a solemn oath to do one's best. As you embrace your 'I AM,' these daily oaths connect you to your mission.

As you fill yourself with beautiful sentiments, maintain a high level of self-belief, recognizing that you embody these qualities as you gaze into the mirror. Look beyond the physical and into the heart of the human being before you, with all the love you can muster. Take each breath deeply and consciously, affirming 'I AM' with each exhale.

Incorporate the following affirmation behind each 'I AM' as you continue on your journey of self-discovery and growth

Show and tell your confident you are courage by embodying these 21 oaths:

"I AM"

- love
- strength
- enriched
- Intelligent
- Peaceful
- Hope
- Courageous
- Joyful
- Humble
- Vulnerable
- Compassionate
- Kind
- Integral
- Faith
- Empathetic
- Forgiveness
- Patience
- flexible
- Imaginative
- neutral
- possible

I know it sounds simple, but building firm confidence is far from simple. It requires inner faith and a commitment to making decisions that best serve our future outcomes. Confidence is not something achieved overnight; it's continual work in progress.

Consistently program your subconscious mind to challenge beliefs surrounding worthiness, self-doubt, and mistaken thinking. On the contrary, by reading books like this one and others that contribute to your personal development, you're taking steps toward success. You're undoubtedly on the right path, so persist in bringing joy to your journey.

8 Knows of Awareness

- I know what I am good at and not good at.
- I know what I know and am gracious when mistaken.
- I know the person I'm becoming even if I don't know when that Person will arrive.
- I know problems are there for me to overcome.
- I know my truth is not everybody truths
- I know what I learn and don't learn take introspections that's start with me.
- I'm willing not to know and still be willing to grow.
- I know to be so im automatically authentic.

The acorn doesn't know why it's planted until it becomes the oak. Wherever you are, trust the process. The ant can move the rubber tree plant without high hopes. The little train that could huffed and puffed with determination. The seven dwarfs whistled as they worked despite differences in confidence and mannerisms. Marvel Studios' Tony Stark character, Ironman, was not just a name; it was an armor made of countless examples of courage that helped him exude confidence.

Even the fictional character and protagonist of Charles Dickens's novel, A Christmas Carol, Ebenezer Scrooge, with some support, changed his bad tidings into good fortune for all to see. Illusions should give you insight into the indeterminate constructs of confidence.

Carbon constitutes 18% of the most common element in the human body. Iron is mixed with carbon to form the alloy known as steel. Iron and steel are in your DNA. That's a fact! Start believing in the bigger, limitless, confident you! Stand tall and fulfill your potential

The Right Stuff

Www.mind.org.uk gives great perspectives on a number of mind topics one I like recently was suggestions on How improve your self-esteem or self-confidence. Here are 5 action steps!

Be advised that different things work for different people at different times.

- Be kind to yourself
- Try to recognize the positives
- Build a support Network
- Try Talking Therapy
- Set yourself a challenge
- Look after yourself

You have likely heard the great vocals of India Arie at some point, and if you haven't, you should, especially the song 'Strength, Courage, and Wisdom' released in 2001 and 'I Am Light' released in 2017.

Both songs are utter masterpieces that carry a testimony of fortitude and self-revelation that these attributes were inside of her. It was elusive until she put a magnifying glass to look deeper.

She said 'stepping out on faith' and 'inside her voice was a soul, in her soul there was a voice.' Imperceptible changes happening inside after listening to the whisper of the soul were the keys to liberate it. It can liberate you too.

That inner voice is something. The ego will fight to keep the territory it knows. Our conscious mind helps us to keep up with the nuances of ourselves and the social workings of the things around us. The ego shouts, the soul whispers. That's how our belief and behavior systems work. We have to believe and conceive like one step in front of the other until walking becomes automatic. So many successes in the past were taken for granted.

When we're at low confidence, we have low awareness, so minor or important things can slip past or over our heads undetected.

High confidence feeling keeps us present, focused, and aware. Sang it, India, strength, courage, and wisdom inside of we!

The right attitude about things comes by way of confidence. Being positive is the calm that happens when the heart has accepted peace of mind. Put aside the things outside of your intrinsic locus of control. As you gain new altitudes, your attitude will improve. Your peak is awaiting you at the top.

Jim Rohn opines that "Happiness is not something you postpone for the future; it is something you design for the present." There is no future and little happiness if you're not every day establishing your confidence.

Personal improvement, relationships (romantic or friendships), social interactions, career growth, association, finances, and all others can be connected to that dominant 'I AM' called confidence.

The confident person has the power to uplift the living from the mundane to the sublime and is able to put triviality behind. Knowing everything is not a prerequisite for having success, only the belief in your infinite possibilities. Be marble, not clay.

Be your own masterpiece, not another's counterfeit. Harness your potential with practice and self-belief. From wherever you're at, do your best. You're that powerful.

"The level of your discipline is in direct correlation to your self-respect."

– Friend, Activist and 8 time
All American Swimmer, Parisa Rose

Feelings & Thoughts

✷ ✷ ✷

CHAPTER EIGHT

Be Not Wise in your Opinion

"Pride is concerned about who's right & humility is concerned about what's right."

– Ezra Taft Benson

"The first half of life is devoted to forming a healthy ego, the second half is going inward and letting go of it"

– Carl Yung

The guru of leadership development, John C. Maxwell, wrote the book 'Sometimes You Win, Sometimes You Learn.' He shares that 'humility is the spirit of learning,' and emphasizes that pride causes people to justify themselves, even when they know they're wrong. He goes on to explain the negative impact that prideful-ness can have on an individual or group: isolation, insecurity, closed-mindedness, blame, denial, and rigidity.

Are you weak in these areas?

You might be wondering how you can improve.

The answer is simple but not a walk in the park: find a good enough reason and commit to practicing the opposite of the aforementioned traits. Discipline over time can nurture any seed into whatever you can imagine whether it leads to good fortune or bad fortune.

Once, I attended an event organized by two friends, where another organizer was also involved. Upon meeting this organizer, I realized we had met before and was excited to see them again.

As I have my own event company, I was confident that some type of collaboration could be worked out for future influencer socials.

However, I was taken aback when they professionally snubbed me. It may have even been unintentional, but it stung, nonetheless. I chose not to turn this sting into a stink.

When your confidence comes from the right place, external events don't control the calm that is ingrained in you. I politely took their information and continued connecting with others, eventually landing two new clients.

I chose to forgive the situation because social cues don't come easily for everyone, and they might not have picked up on their own indiscretion. I didn't let my ego override the empathy I have developed for all people. Humbleness allows you the chance to breathe in between unforeseen circumstances, but only when we don't hold onto the offense.

Don't take these ego spasms personally. People usually don't mean to direct or project their problems onto you; they do it unconsciously to themselves. They are not aware they can practice self-control and never be afflicted with the issues they face daily.

Temperance trumps ego. When you become aware of the things you are ignorant of, then you can be more effective at addressing the underlying sources. That's when we begin the process of becoming consciously conscious or intentionally aware. It's hard not to know a thing. The fact is, we won't know everything there is to know. I'm sure you know that, but do you act like you know that, or is there an ego monster that improvises as you go?

In conversations, we might be tempted to "wing it." We have all done it at some time or another. Our head nods yes, but our brains think, "I will agree to seem sharp." There is no sharpening anything if it results in shame.

Our ego can put us in a bad situation and will if we don't learn how to tame our ego or discipline of delusion. These things break down the capacity to trust who you are and the confident person you are becoming.

"I like you to never to forget that Everything that does not serve your great good gets to be put down or transformed to something utilitarian. Educating the mind without educating the heart is no education at all."

– Aristotle

Have you ever heard the expression humility is a virtue"? One of the most interesting things about mankind is that we are slow to do the things that are good for us while simultaneously too fast in our actions because we think we know a thing. Many bad decisions are made in this fashion.

We claim to know what we don't know or understand, and then we're left wondering where we went wrong. A while ago, I felt compelled to embark on a journey to distinguish between reality and my narrative. I discovered that assumptions, biases, and judgments clouded my perceptions, often leading me to exaggerate my feelings and whether I was wrong or right. Being wise, in my opinion, was acknowledging where I was but not where I wanted to stay.

Why? Let's put it like this: it's impossible to dig yourself out of a ditch that we've created, physically or emotionally. When you're not ready for a realistic examination of why you ended up in a terrible situation, problems arise. In life, we can't properly reflect on adjusting our course if we're not willing to acknowledge what we don't know.

Admitting our ignorance opens the door to curiosity. I put a spin on Confucius's quote, "The person who asks a question is at risk for a moment, the person who does not ask is at risk of their lives." Why did I change it that way? Curiosity is to be taken seriously. It's one of the things we're often discouraged from, especially as children. It is almost beaten out of us during our youth because that's when we are the most inquisitive.

I have a leadership friend in London, Bhavin Shah, who says he is here to instigate the creation and cultivation of more superheroes. He asks questions with the precision of a clockmaker, and he's in good company with Big Ben. In the almost three years of knowing each other, in my opinion, he can't be beaten when it comes to arriving at solutions faster than anyone else.

Besides being curious, it's a rehearsed dance of skill, intuition, and experience. All these attributes start with a humble spirit. If you were to meet him, you would sense those attributes too. I have since given him the nickname 'the Inquisitor,' and anyone like him I meet becomes 'the Inquisitor' as well. The way to find good solutions is to be humble enough to ask good questions. This type of 'good confidence' initiates and transmits empathy, gratitude, and fulfillment. Below are a few things needed to put us back on an even playing field in life;

1. Humbleness takes admitting to yourself not knowing the way out.
2. Support from others that know the way and are willing to show different options.
3. Willingness to listen, learn, respect, reflect, communicate, collaborate, and community.

Let's tackle these 3 concepts:

1. The Meek Shall Inherit The Earth

This concept suggests that the world could be transformed by humble interventions that speak words of peace. Humbleness creates environments characterized by temperance, tolerance, and respect, discouraging petulance, mistreatment, and rash actions. Our words should uplift rather than plague people. As actions should uphold words, a humble nature nurtures a clear perspective. Embracing a positive attitude towards mistakes allows for the creation of new foundations of confidence.

Avoiding Assumptions, Biases, and Judgments (ABDs) requires awareness of when one is engaging in these behavioral vices. Recognizing the undercurrents in which you might have participated signals a lack of acceptance. Embracing humility is essential for receiving awareness.

Understanding awareness involves acknowledging that you don't know what you don't know. We won't comprehend all aspects of most things in our lives; we can only act based on what we know and hope to do so accordingly. None of us are clairvoyant. Forgiving your faults clears the path to 'good Confidence.' This type of confidence is built on both intrinsic and extrinsic compassion. Humility brings you full circle to your self-earnestness.

2. To Know The Road Ahead, Ask Those Coming Back

This Chinese proverb underscores the wisdom of seeking advice from those who have already traversed a path we wish to follow. When embarking on a new endeavor without prior experience or knowledge, it's wise to consult someone who has already taken that journey.

Seeking support from others facilitates a quicker understanding of the way, and it often presents various options to address struggles. Author and motivational speaker Les Brown encapsulates this idea with his quote, "You can see the picture when you're in the frame." By humbly seeking help and receiving constructive responses, we gain valuable insights.

Asking with the belief that we will receive what we seek is crucial, as emphasized in Matthew 7:7-8: *"Ask and it will be given to you; seek and you will find; knock and the door will be opened to you."* Interdependence thrives when a collective of independent individuals supports one another, with no room for know-it-alls. As the axiom from the good book states, "the meek inherit the earth.

3. The willingness to grow takes being new and being ok with that notion.

Shunryu Suzuki quotes, "in the beginner's mind there are many possibilities, in the expert's mind there are few." Your "good confidence" should always be at the patience of your mercies. Keep these with vigilance:

- Listening gives perspective
- Learning gives growth
- Respect give kindness
- Reflection gives introspection
- Communicate gives and builds trust
- Collaboration gives compassion

I only claim what God ordains as mine, No time for pride while I'm on my grind.

"For the foolishness of God is wiser than man's wisdom, and the weakness of God is stronger than man's strength. Brothers, think of what you were when you were called. Not many of you were wise by human standards; not many were influential; not many were of noble birth."

1 Corinthians 1:25-26

To be prideful is a habit that fosters conceitedness, showing arrogant superiority, disdain, haughtiness, and pretentiousness. It often leads to looking down on others, being overbearing, and exhibiting ignorance or annoyance towards them. These traits can be signs of emotional detachment, narcissism, incompetence, immaturity, moral shortcomings, and mistaken self-imposed beliefs. Ultimately, pride can stem from insecurities and/or a lack of self-esteem.

These behaviors slow us down from reaching our full potential. The person who lives with integrity and humility wins and finds greater fulfillment in their life. They have clear aims and are in harmony with themselves because they genuinely love who they are.

Conversely, those who are pitiable drain the life out of themselves and others. They show off but feel empty inside, projecting false confidence that confuses the community. They sow mistrust and mislead others, often engaging in trolling and falling into folly.

Whether they are aware of it or not, it takes a significant amount of energy to maintain this facade, preventing them from being as centered as they could be. Effort turns to error when our lives lack high expectations of ourselves. The good news is that we all have the ability to challenge, change, and grow beyond our past. If you're reading this, that's an awesome first step. Focus on cultivating "the good confidence."

As Jonathan Rauch asserts in "The Happiness Curve," "The river alters the voyager, not just the scenery. Although the world beyond the bend in the river may seem less exciting without an overlay of realistic optimism, it does not appear emptier or narrower. It appears richer and deeper...That is the beginning of wisdom.

The good book talks into the way through the Narrow gate instead of the wide.

Enter through the narrow gate. For wide is the gate and broad is the road that leads to destruction, and many enter through it. But small is the gate and narrow the road that leads to life.

Matthew 7:13-14

Also, the biggest lessons are derived from the maturity that humbles the confidence so not to unintentional pride. Success must be measured cumulatively. That takes being present to your leanings whether virtuous or offensive. I choose to believe in you. Go confidently with the vitality that comes from knowing, believing and doing your own version of virtuousness.

Action and Accountability O'Clock

- Don't let what you know let you think you know it all.
- Write down the good and bad traits you have noticed or people you are often associated with. contributions that come from constructive criticism are needed to support your growth process. Ego or humble.
- Do your best to Embrace yourself with loving patience without (ABD's) every situation.
- your battle doesn't have to be a war. Be willing to persist in working the good habits that lead to the "good confidence".

Feelings & Thoughts

CHAPTER NINE

Choices that Bring Change

In early 2020, like many Americans, I was confronted with the harsh realities of mental, physical, and social issues. As is often the case with significant events in life, it forced us to slow down and reflect on what truly matters. Additionally, the tragic loss of my mother, Eva Rutledge, to heart failure the year before inundated me with a multitude of emotions to navigate.

I could have succumbed to despair, allowing it to color my perspective, or I could have chosen to remain active, redirecting my thoughts to more productive pursuits. Knowing that this is what my mom would have wanted for me, I made the conscious decision to strive for absolution.

Finding solace during times of feeling trapped within our self-imposed purgatory is crucial for processing the insurmountable challenges life presents. For me, it provided a lifeline, though the experience varies for each individual. The burdens of 2019 compounded with the trials of 2020 weighed heavily on my emotional well-being, as we were confined to our respective places.

Towards the end of 2019, an unexpected call from my friend Ayanne offered a form of salvation, guiding me towards a path of transformation through an awareness course. Admittedly, at the time, I had no idea what that entailed.

However, for those familiar with such programs, the profundity of the experience is already understood. It's a journey that requires active participation—it only works if you put in the effort. Such organizations facilitate the expansion of one's mind, providing opportunities to explore new perspectives and insights. It's akin to the choice between the blue or red pill in the Matrix—willingly venturing down the rabbit hole of integrity to uncover truths and build understanding, always keeping the "why" in mind.

I was initially resistant, but with a lukewarm "yes," I made a choice to explore my self-worth. Why was I hesitant, you might ask? In short, the mind only allows us to accept what we have already done; otherwise, it gives us pushback. Unless we are willing to make conscious what we are unconscious about, there is no urgent need for change. The confidence one seeks always gets tested because the conscious mind consistently proves to the subconscious that it's right until the fear of the thing has subsided.

That's what happens when self-belief and self-value validate each other. Collaboration over contrasts starts with us and grows from there, only if we allow it to.

After enrolling in the course, I started to feel anxious because I didn't know what to expect. Despite having limited information, I was assured it would strengthen me as a person.

Two months later, I would experience the clash of the awareness class. While filling out the registration for the online course, a question emerged as a defining moment in my growth journey. It would later become the question I would instruct or coach others to consider in their own growth beginnings. The question was: What were three reasons to participate in this transformative experience? I had to ponder what that meant for me.

I had to confront notions of myself that I hadn't previously considered. I had to be honest about my weaknesses and identify what may have been hindering my growth in various areas of my life. For me, the three answers were working on my procrastination, growing in my pursuit of life, and becoming stronger as a person.

Our relationship with ourselves is often compromised due to a lack of integrity and self-respect. What do I mean, you might ask? It's evident in not finishing an assignment at work, breaking promises to loved ones, becoming increasingly indecisive, struggling to trust others fully, and failing to keep New Year's resolutions.

Jim Rohn puts it like this, "You've been able to side-step the accidents of fate, the quirks of nature, and the innate tendencies we all have to depend on yesterday's solutions to solve today's problems." Complacency arises from not knowing better, so to do better for ourselves. The practice of forgiveness is perhaps the fastest way to reconcile a lack of confidence.

Confidence is the feeling or belief that one can rely on someone or something: firm trust. Self-confidence is a feeling of trust in one's abilities, qualities, and judgment. Without a practice of integrity, one can cut off circulation from intuition, dreams, hope, and self-esteem.

Here are a few experiences of being out of integrity:

- Making a promise to do something but not prioritizing it high enough on the list for whatever reason.
- Failing to follow through on commitments with people.
- Repeatedly failing to keep your word to yourself and others.
- Having a lack of trust in people because you know firsthand the problems caused by not keeping your word.
- Assuming you know what's best for yourself and others without critically analyzing whether it's truth or just your opinion.

- Experiencing inner conflict when a decision needs to be made and practicing indecision as a result.
- Feeling fear when faced with disappointment, dissatisfaction, displeasure, or despair as your plans in life seem to dissipate.
- Not planning for events or special occasions and making excuses for why you didn't show up.

Change will happen with or without our control; that's a fact. During these times in life, it can help to be prepared, prudent, and patient. Prudent with our choices. Prepared with decision-making.

The other day, while posting on the platform formerly known as Twitter, now known as "X," I came across a wise connector's post that said, "God has already prepared the way; He is just preparing you." Be patient with ourselves once the decision is made.

Epistemology, the theory of knowledge, especially with regard to its methods, validity, and scope, explores what distinguishes justified belief from opinion. Epistemology suggests that knowledge comes in two forms: we can know "declared knowledge" and understand "procedural knowledge."

Brian Tracy outlines "The Four D's to a Successful Life" as follows:

- Desire
- Decision (getting off the fence)
- Discipline

- Determination

"When you're not sure, flip a coin because when that coin is in the air, you realize which one you're actually hoping for."

– Arnold Rothstein

Confidence is rooted in the realizations and repetitions of your experiences, as well as in the ways you expand your capabilities. It's the belief that you can do something again, even if you don't recall doing it in a similar way before. Consistently practicing awareness helps build mantras that align with our principles. Here are some acronyms to remember and keep highlighted in your life to encourage you to "go for what you want" in your day-to-day:

Take your S.H.O.T

- Sharing -your intentions
- Hope -is never giving up
- Optimism -is open to the possibilities & embrace them
- Trust -in the process & the connecting with people that can bring the vision into fruition.

Our daily A.P.P.L.E.E keeps us growing:

Awareness
Presence
Patience
Learning
Earnest
Empathy

Taking these acronyms to heart through repetition will undoubtedly lead to an increase in confidence.

Remember, you only expand in what you will achieve with intention and intensity. Repetition serves as the main driver for imprinting your intentions in your mind, so it's crucial to be attentive to what you are saying to yourself.

The way we use and structure our words can transform a lion into a cat or a cat into a lion. Therefore, carefully choosing our words and consistently reinforcing positive affirmations can empower us to achieve remarkable feats.

Feelings & Thoughts

____

____

____

____

____

____

____

____

____

____

____

____

____

CHAPTER TEN

The Way of A.G.A.P.E is a Legacy

"Leaders are dealers in hope"
– **Napoleon Bonaparte**

"Why should you stay at the bottom of a well when there's a strong rope in your hands."
– **Rumi**

It's a divine law of oneness, a remarkable revelation of our interconnectedness. I've come to understand and deeply resonate with the idea that we're all part of a greater whole in the world, like individual threads intricately woven into an immense cosmic tapestry.

Our thoughts, actions, and emotions reverberate through this tapestry, influencing not just ourselves but also others and the world around us. Each thought and action we contribute sets off a series of effects, whether seen or unseen. In this context, agape love emerges as the pinnacle of our actions. Agape, from the Greek language, embodies a universal love and compassion that transcends boundaries and encompasses all.

While you are living out your more confident self, always pay that type of confidence forward to others. There is a gospel group called commissioned that has a song that says, "Love isn't love till you given it away… Love isn't love until you are willing to give it to somebody else." How true!

Confidence has a meaning and then a mission

In 2021, I initiated a leadership club on the Clubhouse app. At that time, it served as an international platform where eager and capable individuals could engage in thought-provoking discussions led by polymaths on a variety of important topics. While not all discussions were strictly intellectual, the environment fostered a sense of intellectualism that appealed to many. Users could navigate through the "hallways," seeking out rooms where they could participate in conversations aligned with their interests.

Recognizing that there were limited options for social interaction, particularly in the United States, I saw Clubhouse as a valuable outlet for fostering connection.

I believed that strong leadership had the power to uplift individuals and inspire confidence.

By connecting our present circumstances to our future potential, we could cultivate the connections we desired with confidence in our ability to thrive. It became evident to me that we could grow by remaining attuned to the possibilities on the horizon.

These "event horizons" are moments that define, challenge, or shape us. They represent opportunities for growth and can serve as pivotal moments for personal reinvention. My vision for the leadership club was to create a safe space where individuals could come together to share their voices, ideas, and perspectives, contributing to a collective sense of empowerment and belief in each other's potential.

The rising of our words will enable tranquil thought that can inspire new perspective- Arthur J Rutledge

A new horizon for me is called A.G.A.P.E legacies.

Let's give an **A.G.A.P.E** breakdown:

AWARENESS

At the outset of each chapter in my leadership journey, uncertainty cast a large shadow. Setting forth, I reached out to others without a clear map of what lay ahead. Along the way, I unexpectedly morphed into a more attentive listener, a compassionate sharer, an empathetic organizer, a beacon of positivity, an intentional inspirer, a trusted confidant, a visionary for teams, a captain of mindset, and an enthusiastic motivator. None of these roles were foreseen, yet they naturally unfurled as I engaged with people, expressing my genuine desire to support and uplift those who sought to be heard.

I began by connecting with individuals one by one, unaware of the ripple effect that would follow. Each interaction led to another, creating a chain reaction as individuals shared their experiences with others. Through this process, I discovered that when you exude confidence in yourself, your message resonates with that same confidence. Your actions become as fervent as your dreams, enabling you to overcome any fear that may arise.

Furthermore, cultivating awareness provides an endless wellspring of clarity and enriches your personal insights into life. By staying attuned to your surroundings and experiences, you gain valuable perspective that guides your path forward with purpose and conviction.

GROWTH

Prioritizing personal development has been my focus for the past decade, and it has truly brought out the best in me. Achieving growth requires nothing more than dedicating some time and effort.

You might find it amusing to think about your own journey towards growth, perhaps realizing it's been less than 10 years for you. Or maybe you're already on that path.

Regardless, growth entails various elements: maturing, correcting habits, being kind to yourself during the process of unlearning and relearning, adapting to changing circumstances, understanding the importance of timing, nurturing a desire for learning, maintaining patience through shifts in mindset, seeking guidance from mentors and coaches, setting and pursuing goals, trusting the process, finding a rhythm, managing emotions, maintaining consistency, and the list goes on.

The great news is that as you embark on this intentional journey of self-improvement, you'll begin to experience joy from the progress you make, reaching a point where you no longer count the days. Eventually, growth becomes a natural part of who you are, and your actions reflect your inner development. Just as trees, fruits, birds, or stars don't measure time, neither should we.

Embrace growth from wherever you are, and once you've mastered that mindset, fulfillment will follow. Have faith in your efforts, knowing they will lead you to the lessons you need to excel, while leaving behind excuses and embracing authenticity.

ALTRUISM

Altruism, as defined, embodies an unselfish concern for the well-being of others, exemplified through charitable acts motivated purely by altruistic intentions. It's about extending a helping hand without expecting anything in return. This concept resonates deeply with the principle of Ubuntu, a term originating from African philosophy, which emphasizes the interconnectedness of humanity. As Desmond Tutu eloquently expressed, "My humanity is bound up in yours, for we can only be human together."

Tutu frequently championed the idea of human unity, emphasizing the power of mutual care and collective respect. His advocacy for Ubuntu helped to bridge divides and foster harmony in fractured societies. Altruism, then, becomes a powerful expression of solidarity, a testament to our faith in one another, and a compassionate gesture paid forward.

For me, the mantra "sharing is caring" encapsulates the essence of altruism. By cultivating gratitude, appreciation, and forgiveness, I find myself feeling more whole and fulfilled. This sense of abundance enables me to give generously and perpetually, fueled by a well-centered and considerate heart. Such actions require bravery, sacrifice, servitude, humility, and trust – qualities that emanate from a place of conscious confidence.

PURPOSE

The scholar and philosopher Friedrich Nietzsche offered profound insights into the importance of acting with purpose, stating, "I know of no better life purpose than to perish in attempting the great and impossible." Nietzsche challenges the notion that something being deemed impossible should deter us from pursuing it.

On the contrary, he argues that the very fact of its impossibility makes it worth pursuing. For Nietzsche, courage and greatness stem from facing uncertainty and embracing risk. He suggests that without these challenges, there would be no opportunity for courage to manifest itself. In his view, the only true failure lies in shrinking away from life's challenges, rather than boldly confronting them.

"He who has a why to live can bear almost any how." This powerful statement, attributed to Friedrich Nietzsche, underscores the importance of having a clear purpose in life. Similarly, the words of Rumi resonate deeply: "Let what you love be what you do." For me, fulfilling the passion of the heart has always been a guiding light, despite the countless hours of hard work, setbacks, and disappointments along the way.

Indeed, a purpose without perseverance is merely an empty shell. We often speak of and yearn for happiness, but it is a well-conceived purpose that truly brings a smile to our faces. It instills within us a sense of determination, sustains us in times of difficulty, fuels our creativity, and drives our industriousness. Moreover, it calms our fears and uncertainties, offering the blessed assurance that we are supported by a higher power.

Those who succeed in life are not merely passive recipients of circumstance; they actively seek out the circumstances they desire, and if they cannot find them, they create them. It all begins with a burning desire, unwavering self-belief, and a clear understanding of what one wants. Decisiveness is the antidote to aimlessness, and building confidence around a deeply rooted purpose can smooth the path ahead, making the journey that much more manageable.

ENTHUSIASM

Build your life around your abilities, gifts, strengths, or talents. Enthusiasm, while essential, is fleeting on its own. It requires discipline and a strong support system to sustain it. While new ideas and endeavors can keep energy flowing initially, the day-to-day grind can eventually take its toll. It's crucial to find imaginative ways to keep the fire burning, even when things start to feel routine.

You know what gets you excited, but it's important to approach excitement with moderation and create good disciplines around it. As the seven dwarves in Snow White knew well, collaborative enthusiasm can maximize effectiveness. Just as they worked together harmoniously, you too can leverage the power of teamwork and synergy.

Concentration is key when working towards any goal. Dreams require the appropriate amount of focus, attention to detail, and reflection to adhere to lessons learned and achieve moments of clarity. By maintaining focus and dedicating yourself to your goals, you can set yourself up for success and bring your dreams to fruition.

The aspiration of The A.G.A.P.E Legionaries is to provide a motivationally driven, introspective overview aimed at increasing creative agility and transforming complacent thinking. Through inspirational communication, we seek to cultivate connections that empower individuals to transcend the mundane and reach the sublime.

In today's ever-growing societies, global connection is paramount. To uphold this truth, it behooves us to consciously move forward despite folly and continuously rise to the occasion. By constructing a process of trustworthiness within ourselves first, we pave the way for meaningful connections and lasting impact.

Our mindset is centered on internal growth, which in turn enables us to emerge as leaders capable of guiding others. We recognize the value of strength in vulnerability and gain wisdom through our evaluated experiences of both success and failure.

I believe that the leadership cultivated in those rooms, where we met 3-4 times a week for up to 5 hours at a stretch, over the course of 2 years and with close to 17,000 members, will inevitably have a profound impact on our society at large. These champions courageously stepped up, despite feeling unconcerned, uncomfortable, intimidated, insecure, and vulnerable, in order to expand their perspectives in unexpected ways.

I was once in the same boat as them, and they graciously extended their patience and respect to me. In return, I offered them my heart and undivided attention.

For a select few, this experience fostered a sense of familial belonging—a feeling of home. In living abundantly, these integral parts that make us whole in life are surrounded by people who are willing to nurture, support, and renew relationships.

A confident individual should always be open to connecting and contributing. When you have a clear direction of who you want to be, reaching out to others opens doors to endless pursuits of value in the world.

I believe that God's ultimate love, known as "AGAPE," manifests in the tests we endure to bring out the best in ourselves in life. Achieving consistency in self-resilience and self-trust requires abundant patience and love. It's not just about trusting yourself but also instilling trust in others.

When you possess the ability to do this almost instantly, you pave the way for new connections during the exploration of the soul, such as self-value. The value you make available to yourself eventually translates into trust. It's essential to cultivate this trust sooner rather than later, as any trust should be leveraged to compensate for lost intentions.

Your aim should be to compound in confidence, seeking returns on investment in relationships or revenue. While risks are real, so are losses. Persist in growing stronger, and you will reap gains. Developing confidence involves taking risks, knowing that it leads to freedom.

Confidence in decision-making expands your horizons, whether it's in relationships, exploring new places, or pursuing opportunities. These are all events waiting for your engagement in life. Grand experiences that suit your tastes stem from the connections you make, and this freedom grows valuable and multiplies with perseverance.

To maintain self-trust while aligning with your future self and maintaining a healthy outlook, I recommend focusing on three key aspects to strengthen confidence and enhance connections.

Put Your Trust To The Test

This is a concept and philosophy I had to practice long before I developed a strong sense of confidence. Growing up, I was popular but not notable. It wasn't until after high school that I truly found my footing in life, and even before then, I wasn't as noticeable. My trust in people was, at best, tolerant for a while. I believe in God's mercies because I believe He sprinkled people in my life who saw the best in me and went above and beyond, showing me what I consider to be agape love.

When you reach a place where you embrace life's obstacles and obligations, it fosters an unbeatable spirit. This type of trust must be earned to prepare for life's unexpected challenges. Embracing your tests as treasures will make your trust tremendous.

Believing in others will reveal how much you truly trust yourself. How we relate to ourselves is directly correlated to how we treat others. Self-trust is a sign that we care and believe in ourselves.

I wrote this book because I care about you, drawing from over 40 years of blood, sweat, tears, and jeers to build my self-efficacy. It certainly didn't happen overnight, and some of us have more heavy lifting to do to find pleasant pastures. But underneath it all, we are all from and on the same ground.

Trust is a voyage, not an arrival. It guides us sometimes without a clear direction. Trust is a friend when lonely and an uncertain ally in turmoil. Like the confidence we seek, self-trust can be an adversary. However, I can guarantee that if you trust yourself more than you don't, you will become a person of substance and gain the intuition to navigate through storms victoriously.

Put Your Curiosity To The Test.

Put the pedal to the medal & to reach your destination swiftly, ask more questions. Whether you're met with rejection or reward, the act of questioning will lead you closer to understanding. Remember, even a "no" is a form of solution, guiding you towards what is, isn't, or what could be.

Every path leads somewhere and embracing curiosity means being agile enough to navigate the obstacles along the way. As Henry Ford once said, "Obstacles are those frightful things you see when you take your eyes off your goal." Indeed, without a clear direction, there can be no goal. So, embrace the challenge of being personable and sociable. Transform any apprehension into creative energy, crafting a new narrative that leads to better outcomes.

The journey towards becoming adept at asking quality questions begins by stepping out of your comfort zone. Start by addressing the questions you've been afraid to ask yourself. True earnestness starts with self-awareness. If you find yourself struggling or deeply triggered, consider seeking guidance from a qualified psychologist.

Remember, you undergo a process of self-discovery every year. Curiosity is already in practice! Our thoughts and sensibilities constantly evolve due to the myriad experiences we encounter. Therefore, it's crucial to foster a mindset conducive to growth and positivity.

Above all, never shy away from confronting yourself. Embrace your best self with both attention and intention. Stay confident in your curiosity, for it holds the key to unlocking new opportunities and deeper understanding.

Put Your Commitment To The Test.

Throughout this book, I've emphasized the advantages of living without restrictions and remaining steadfast in your confidence. Central to this journey is self-trust and sustainable curiosity. True commitment is demonstrated by consistently investing effort in the right areas until genuine techniques are developed.

Progress towards a goal requires diligence and foresight, ensuring that each step taken aligns with the overarching objective. Keeping track of your progress is vital for maintaining determination. This includes setting benchmarks, celebrating small victories, establishing accountability partnerships, and prioritizing tasks based on urgency.

Integrity check-ups are crucial to ensure alignment between actions and intentions, while actively avoiding negative distractions and self-destructive thoughts reinforces commitment to your cause. Repetition is key; reinforcing positive habits and mindset shifts will solidify your commitment to growth and development.

Engaging in activities you love and leveraging your talents are important, but it's your ability to remain present and dedicated that truly matters. As the music group Salt-N-Pepa famously sang, "Express yourself, you've got to be you and only you, baby!" So, let's embrace our journey with confidence and determination, rocking both mind and body along the way.

Leadership expert and mentor of thought, John C. Maxwell, famously declares, "Life begins at the end of our comfort zone. We go there by stretching ourselves. Let's stretch and prepare for the best version of ourselves! Legacy is what you make it. What legacy will you leave behind?

Many of us shy away from embracing the qualities that could propel us to great heights. Throughout my journey, I've encountered various types of leaders, but the truly impactful ones all share a common trait. They didn't necessarily think or believe they were leaders; instead, they either had to be told or naturally rose to the occasion. They were authentic individuals who continually developed their skills along the way. These leaders exuded strength of character, which spoke volumes more than any title or position they held. Over time, they were recognized and uplifted by others as true leaders.

As confidence grows, so do our abilities. By being fully open to ourselves, we develop the emotional empathy needed to be open to others. This aligns with the law of oneness that I've explored throughout this chapter, emphasizing our interconnectedness and shared humanity.

Embracing the right philosophy in life can be as simple as the establishing of words to support yourself in reaching your goals. Earn your mastery through loving patience and relentless repetition.

Let these words by William Arthur Ward become an instrument to express encouragement throughout your life:

The word "leadership" encompasses much more than just guiding others—it's primarily about leading oneself. It requires a unique commitment to honoring one's own nature. Each individual is crafted with their own distinctiveness for a purposeful existence.

Through introspection and intrinsic control, you gain mastery over the ideas and narratives shaping your story. Only when you fully embrace this concept do you become the hero of your own narrative. Your mission isn't impossible; it's innate and even inevitable when coupled with self-belief and agape love. As your understanding aligns with your passion, your potential will seamlessly merge with its purpose. Your AGAPE legacy awaits, ready to be fulfilled.

Feelings & Thoughts

CHAPTER ELEVEN

The Confidence Called Courage

"Courage doesn't happen when you have all the answers. It happens when you are ready to face the questions you have been avoiding your whole life."
– Shannon L. Alder

"Nature loves courage. You make the commitment and nature will respond to that commitment by removing impossible obstacles."
– Terrance McKenna

"The courage of Living is the confidence to take action, and Step past the knowing into the doing"
– Arthur J Rutledge

How much more could you experience by stepping out of your comfort zone and facing your fears regularly? How much better would you feel about yourself? And how much more impact could you create in people's lives?

In truth, no human being has ever fully explored their potential. We have infinite room to grow. We are the only species on Earth with the power of imagination, which can alter the course of our own destiny.

To unlock our capacity for growth, we must cultivate the unexpected courage that arises from new experiences. We have the opportunity to move beyond our comfort zone, one day at a time, one step at a time."

"My mother always used to tell me the story of how I started getting out of my comfort zone, which, for most of us, began with a baby crib. I was an early walker; my clever 9-month-old self would wait until no one was watching and attempt my escape into whatever room I was in at the time. I have always been a curious person, and these escapades were adventures that I would or wouldn't attempt at different times.

Whether it was crawling over the top of the crib inspired by laughter from the next room, noises from pets outside, or my favorite sounds of music, I was always on the move. My mom often said I could dance before I could walk, and that held true too—I'm still a dancing machine, but only when the mood strikes. Most of the time, I didn't successfully make it over the top of the crib, but whether I fell, bounced, cried, or laughed it off, I was never dissuaded from trying again. While I don't remember most of those moments, I do know that I'm still braving the falls in life, just as you are."

Baby feet, baby steps. Adult feet, bigger steps. Our journey of personal growth is defined by our awareness of what we can achieve. It is our deepest desires that leave the most profound imprint and wield the widest impact.

Denis Waitley once remarked, "Roots and wings are more important than loot and things." This underscores the fundamental importance of establishing a solid foundation rooted in our core beliefs and values.

It is this foundation that provides us with the wings to soar to new heights, unencumbered by material pursuits.

By adhering steadfastly to these foundational principles, we fortify our self-belief, creating an unshakable resilience that enables us to weather any storm that life may throw our way. Through daily reaffirmation of these principles, we stay resolute in our pursuit of our dreams, always mindful of the path we have chosen and the destination that awaits us.

Consistency in our actions, whether in the formative years of youth or the seasoned maturity of adulthood, serves as the yardstick by which we measure our growth and self-respect. It is through this unwavering commitment to our principles that we cultivate an unwavering strength of purpose, enduring patience, and a boundless courage that knows no bounds.

Conversely, the neglect of these foundational principles can lead to a life marred by timidity, indifference, and a lack of vision. It is only by fully embracing these principles that we can unleash our true potential and rise to the challenges that lie before us.

Confidence, the cornerstone of our journey, begins with a firm belief in our abilities and a steadfast commitment to realizing our full potential. It is through this unwavering faith in ourselves that we embark on the path to greatness, guided by the beacon of courage that burns brightly within us.

As we embrace discomfort and venture outside our comfort zones, our confidence naturally grows, expanding our horizons and propelling us towards ever greater heights of achievement. What once seemed insurmountable becomes mere steppingstones on our path to success.

In the journey towards self-mastery, gaining control over our emotions is paramount. As we harness the power of our emotions, our confidence blossoms, radiating outward and inspiring those around us to reach for their own dreams.

So let us take to heart the words of Thibaut Meurisse, "Success is inevitable." For when we believe in ourselves and embrace the journey with unwavering confidence, there is no limit to what we can achieve."

- Confidence is built by creatively facing what you fear.

- Confidence says, "I will be fine no matter what others say."
- Confidence is knowing your place is wherever you're present.
- Confidence involves taking slow steps at the beginning and then taking leaps.
- Confidence, like happiness, comes in waves.
- Confidence is the process you undertake by being conscious and persistent in what you say to yourself.
- Confidence occurs when you are intentionally passionate about what you are becoming and kind to yourself about the areas in which you are growing.
- Confidence stems from realizing that you display it every day by doing what you said you were going to do, even after the initial volition or emotion has passed. Integrity always gets reborn, rebuilt, and rewarded.
- Admiring someone is great but remember that you are standing close enough to observe the same thing in yourself. Your trust or lack thereof comes directly from your confidence.
- If you are unsure of your self-confidence level, you must be persistent in moving forward during moments of doubt.

Go, champion!

L.E.A.P towards your possibilities by learning these easy 4 step disciplines:

Learn
Effective
Action
Principles

Learning to be effective with action principles will take from ground to sky only if you take the L.E.A.P's In your life.

Author and business guru Brian Tracy suggests, "Always concentrate on the most valuable use of your time. This is what separates the tamed assertive from the vain intentioned. Self-esteem is the reputation you have with yourself."

Every day, we can excel in all that's in our hearts to do. By prioritizing these tasks first, we maintain integrity with ourselves, and excellence becomes readily accessible. Ralph Waldo Emerson quoted, "Nothing is at last sacred but the integrity of your own mind. Envy is ignorance, imitation is suicide. Trust thyself: every heart vibrates to that iron string." He also said, "Our greatest glory is not in never failing, but in rising up every time we fail. With the past, I have nothing to do, nor with the future. I live now." Find your iron string and stay true to it. Go out and meet confidence head-on. Deep inside, you know why you want to live boldly. People are curious about your uniqueness, and you can only discover it by showcasing the beauty within you in a spectacular way.

Furthermore, know that we only truly grow by sharpening each other. If you find yourself thinking, "I like being alone," and if you're sure that's all to your life story, then live your truth until you decide otherwise. However, this is only to emphasize that having the confidence to live boldly is as valuable as that yellow brick road. It's a blessing to take on the world in a new and fresh way, rather than sitting at home and letting precious time drift away.

Decide to believe that your conditions in life are molding you into the strength and actions you admire in another. That effort grows & improves from the will to do by its repetition. I admire many people that are there because they desired to improve me.

There are Mentors and friends that have inspired me indirectly and directly like: explorer/historian Sturla Ellingvag, John C. Maxwell, Brendon Burchard, Karim R. Ellis, Earl Nightingale, Marie Forleo, Jim Rohn, Kevin McGovern, Bob Proctor, Wayne W. Dyer, Deepak Chopra, Don Miguel Ruiz, Eric Thomas, Stephen R. Covey, Carl Jung, Rumi, Marcus Aurelius, Socrates, Martin Meadows, Brianna Wiest, Rachel Luna, Anthony Robins, Vernon Davis, Dale Carnegie, Napoleon Hill, Bill Bellamy, Eddie Murphy, MLM guru's Patrick and Michael Maser, singing phenomenon's Isaac & Thorald

Koren, Stevie Wonder, franchise magnet Richie Romero, entrepreneurs past & present and beats goes on as the singing group the whispers would say.

That may leave you out of breath, but it only started with a couple then a few more. 10 plus years later of being consistent does multiple.

Confidence doesn't fall from the sky; you get to be the eagle that's in flight. Each of the above individuals went for what they wanted, even without the confidence they have today. Whether it's through books, seminars, courses, inspirational associations, knowledgeable mentors, curious constructive coaching, or you as a new leader exhibiting courage to others, remember to keep moving confidently while putting the right people in your life. Help people find their voice in a way that gives them footing, thereafter developing wings. You can only perform as confidently as your confidence allows.

You only play as your confidence let's you. If you're very confident, you can do anything.

– Arthur Ashe

"Whatever you do, you need courage. Whatever course you decide upon, there is always someone to tell you that you are wrong. There are always difficulties arising that tempt you to believe your critics are right."

– Ralph Waldo Emerson

Levels from timid to confidence:

- Dismayed - pity, blame, disheartened
- Critical - judgment, excuses & state of doubt
- Aligned/ Affirming - ambivalent/neutral/moments of self-belief
- Agreeable -open to possibly/optimistic /
- Assertive - aspiring & reciprocating
- Self efficacy/ - nurturing/ wholeness

"Courage is knowing what not to fear,"

– Plato.

"We have so many pieces to ourselves that searching them out can leave us uncertain at times. Only when we endure with patience to connect them do we create wonder and a sense of wholeness. 'Aplomb' is a word I found that describes a person having self-confidence, poise, or self-assurance, especially when in a demanding situation."

17 ways to be an APLOMB person:

- Find or create exercise that will grow you in trusting yourself.
- Stand tall even if you feel low.
- Be Lovingly Patience with ourselves on any encounter or endeavor.

- Staying kind to add yourself and others with thoughtful words and actions.
- Create and practice new things.
- Find optimism in every situation.
- Always talk up with assurance.
- Don't dwell on what you can't do but what you're able to become.
- Take initiative in the aspects of life you know and have interest in often.
- If you tell yourself a negative thought replace it with 2-3 positive ones.
- Groove with groups that are confident.
- Smile through discomfort.
- Find something to celebrate even on those difficult days.
- Write down 10 or more things that you achieved at the end of every week to remind yourself of your importance and potential.
- Read books that emphasize empowering yourself.
- Find mentors or coaches.
- Grow emotional agility through the practice of meeting new people and experiencing new things.

In summary, I'm not suggesting bungee jumping or becoming a bull rider. Unless those are legitimately what you want to do. Let's explore the joy of embracing new experiences. Remember, stepping out of your comfort zone is where life's greatest rewards lie. Like the saying goes, 'the apple is always at the end of the limb.'

Let's embark on a journey of self-discovery and confidence-building, where every step forward is a celebration of our worth and potential. With unwavering confidence, we become the architects of our destiny, shaping our reality through bold action and fearless determination. Let's channel the spirit of the brave child within us, who fearlessly climbs, walks, and runs towards their dreams.

Embrace the power of action, for every stumble is a step closer to success. Let's live fully, believing in ourselves and our ability to overcome any obstacle. It's not about being ready or waiting for the perfect moment – it's about seizing the present and making the most of every opportunity.

Let's commit to living our best lives, filled with courage, confidence, and boundless optimism. Whether we're introverts or extroverts, confidence is the key that unlocks the door to freedom and endless possibilities.

Feelings & Thoughts

Epilogue

"Wherever you go, go with all your heart"
~ **Confucius**

"Never forget that the greatest reward of pursuing a dream is who you become as a result."
~ **John C. Maxwell**

"The only limit to our realization of tomorrow will be our doubts of today."
~ **Franklin D. Roosevelt**

Life … is about not knowing, having to change, taking the moment and making the best of it, without knowing what's going to happen next. Delicious ambiguity.
– **Gilda Radner**

I made myself smile every day until it became automatic. I made myself laugh every day until I appreciated the little details of life. I danced every day while an adolescent so no bad feeling could hold me down as an adult. Peace is held for a period by the person that doesn't see the direction of where they go, but a person that makes peaceful moments is in hopes of better also awakened with the idea of who a person will become.

Author and spiritual leader Marianne Williamson said, "The purpose of our lives is to give birth to the best that is in us. It is only through our own personal awakening that the world can be awakened. We cannot give what we do not have."

Knowing and breathing with full use of our lungs, acting with every beat of our heat, and finding living to the fullest desire of our souls. Living without a mask, effulgently! What does the future of a person with a confident outlook accomplish...everything they want! to do that you always get to remain a person that checks in the mirror of your soul and inquires what will make you the most complete person you can become. To ask an age-old question, what is to become of yourself if you don't listen to your heart? For the majority of you who are reading this book regret is a land that you have been living in for years.

FOMO (feeling of missing out) will be a weekly assurance if you don't start acting on your behalf to remedy the feelings of living or succeeding up to what the master of the universe deems you capable. Gaby Bernstein suggests this affirmation to get in touch with self; "I am willing to let go of my self-doubt. I surrender to self-love…" she goes on to explain, "Whenever we place our happiness and peace in anything outside of ourselves, we'll inevitably feel unfulfilled and stuck. trust that every second you choose a new perspective is a miracle."

Live life as the gift it is without past or future to aggravate your experience. We are the most valuable material isn't on the periodic table or in the deep on the ocean's floor. It's not like the end of the rainbow or at the end of the yellow brick road. It's not on moon or growing on mars.

It's not in the streets of any city or on a mountain high. It's not Buried in deep a garden or discovered in irrigated acres. It's not in your might, fight, flight or trite of things external. The owning of your Value can only be gained, expressed, measured, and meaningful through what your heart seeks and is willing to find. John C. Maxwell concluded that, "Confidence is preparation. When opportunity knocks, it's too late to prepare."

Follow the pieces that are given to you in this book as the bread crumbs to success and the things that you found puzzling will become complete. Make sure you practice patient trust in your experience.

Prosperity comes from the preparation of the hope that you aspire towards. Self-belief helps you to succeed in that hope. If your heart has high hopes of winning then a clear, confirmed, courageous confidence will get you there!

To transmogrify our lives and experience who we are becoming will take putting your best you forward and not in forgot.

A Transformation of yourself needs a transition in beliefs, behaviors and values. These don't just occur by happenstance but are preserved by the priorities you set on following through with committed effort.

"We see the body acting out the minds dramas but where is the director who decides which scene comes next"

– Deepak Chopra.

It might be true that Life is more than what's going on that's out of our control. The most important thing we can do is become intrinsically stronger. That's mostly done from the heart to the mind. To combat the minimal programmed instincts that our externally ego driven thinking & actions.

Inner Peace is the best thing to accomplish first, then work from that good space to be consciously proactive in the world. The world will be going on long after us. In the now make your serenity your sanctuary.

"The brighter the light the darker the shadow"

– Carl J. Jung

I found this while on the mission to talk into confident courage by Thomas Fowell Buxton. It's goes, "The longer I live, the more I am certain that the great difference between men – between the feeble and the powerful, the great and the insignificant; is energy, invincible determination, a purpose once fixed, and then – death or victory! That quality will do anything that can be done in this world, and no talents, no circumstances, no opportunities, will make a two-legged creature a man without it."

Charlie Chaplin Once observed and became principled in these....

"As I began to love myself
I found that anguish and emotional suffering
are only warning signs that I was living against
my own truth.
Today, I know, this is Authenticity.
As I began to love myself
I understood how much it can offend somebody
if I try to force my desires on this person, even though
I knew the time was not right and the person was not
ready for it,
and even though this person was me.
Today I call this Respect.
As I began to love myself
I stopped craving for a different life, and I
could see that everything that surrounded me
was inviting me to grow.
Today I call this Maturity.
As I began to love myself
I quit stealing my own time,
and I stopped designing huge projects
for the future.

Today, I only do what brings me joy and happiness,
things I love to do and that make my heart cheer,
and I do them in my own way
and in my own rhythm.
Today I call this Simplicity.
As I began to love myself
I freed myself of anything
that is no good for my health –
food, people, things, situations,
and everything that drew me down and away from
myself.
At first, I called this attitude a healthy egoism.
Today I know it is Love of Oneself.
As I began to love myself
I quit trying to always be right,
and ever since I was wrong less of the time.
Today I discovered that is Modesty.
As I began to love myself

I recognized that my mind could disturb me and it can
make me sick. But as I connected it to my heart, my
mind became a valuable ally. Today I call this connec-
tion Wisdom of the Heart.
We no longer need to fear arguments, confrontations or
any kind of problems with ourselves or others. Even stars
collide, and out of their crashing, new worlds are born.

Today I know: This is Life!"

I have put you several steps closer to confidence ascendancy. The ability to measure how influential you will be is in the palm of your hands. Read this book as much as you need. The lesson we learn at different times in our lives can catapult our development in ways we can't consciously conceive. Create a crest of Avidity that will bring you closer to your best self and share it without hesitation to others that need confidence the most. Nothing can stop or subdue you if you don't let your light dull. I have been short on confidence, and I give you this from a place of agape. Your truest success happens by knowing and walking in your worth. Value your value.

Shine on!

Acknowledgements

We are never an army of me. Even if we initiate an idea, it doesn't come to fruition without a team. My confidence is in you for a better tomorrow.

Business director at the LA Tribune Alisha Magnus-Louis with your big heart for putting me in the right position to shine.

Director of Publishing at LA Tribune Pattie Godfrey~Sadler and New Life Clarity Publishing for bring my love by way of this book to the masses. You and your leadership mission rock!

The John C. Maxwell team (JMT) organization for helping me sharpen my speaking, coaching, & training skills.

The Altru Center family for setting me on the path to strength of excellence and being the change I want to be in the world. I know what transformative awareness and alignment is because of your mastermind courses.

The way you are at stand breaths confidence and joy into every heart you reach.

To **Bobby Kennedy** for reintroducing me to learning by giving me the gift of your belief in me in the form of a book to show that I was MORE.

Nadia Hussey-Vidal for not only proofreading the book but being an emotional rock during this first book growth journey.

Ayanne Harrison, Basil Hamadeh, Nicholas Monarch for being powerful figures of strength in times I needed reminding of my infinite possibilities.

To **Katherine Norland & Jaiden Kane** for that great talk on that faithful day in Atlanta that enhanced the vision for my book. those constructive criticisms challenged me to go deeper into my book finishing mission.

Giada Bardelli not only my book's graphic designer, but she is also the new author of (Not A Princess - The Journal) and CEO of G.J Attitude apparel. Despite her being from fresh from Italy she has inspired me. How much harder did she have it and still able to keep strong in spite of going through the obvious and also the unknown. Still confident, still shining. Thank you!

To **Tinashe Mudiwa** host of By Product of Will and Grace podcast Thought leader & Yaba Sims-Erwiah **Dance/Aerobics Instructor for your great advice and**

needed constructive criticisms. Thank you for the valuable input.

My clubhouse A.G.A.P.E legacies club/house that have cultivated and inspired me more than you all could ever know. You all have and are making the world a most wonderful place:

Parisa Rose author,8x national swim champion all American, and integrity Leader.

Dr. Karim R. Ellis author of (GPS your success), motivational speaker, And host of the Les brown motivational show.

Dr. Alisa Whyte the #1 mindset disruptor/ speaker/ entrepreneur

Janice M. Colman author of (the 26 doses of career triage), speaker and high-performance career coach.

Dr. Dyerek Harris author/veteran/professor

Femala Fleming author of "Your Body is a Multi-Million Dollar Corporation Act Like It", total fitness coach, and speaker. Their Website can be found at eqfitnessgroup.com

Janine Bensouda thought leader and peace crusader.

Brad Melnychuk fitness coach and speaker.

Tammi Spearman speaker/imagineer of purpose/ entrepreneur

Megan Kettl motivational speaker/ suicide prevention advocate

Tom Macomber Life and Leadership Consultant.

Jeff Massone executive business coach and thought leader.

Alex Garzaro Women's confidence coach and speaker.

Joseph Kim entrepreneur, speaker, and faith spreader.

Fred Wachter ministry of music and inner strength consular.

Zein Virani leadership and mindset speaker

Ella Matheson peace ambassador of peace in the city, mystical thought leader, and ESG impact investor.

Ashton Cantou executive coach and wellness advocate

Trena Bolden fields author of (from idea to six figures) and

Bhavin Shah confidence coach and master knowledge inquisitor

Brian Penso author of (who are you & why?) and entrepreneur

Brianah Kirtley professional speaker and artist avant

Angela and Knittels Ansa owners of career oasis & aspire prosthetics/orthotics

Leadership Accelerator Workshop | Career Oasis & Prosthetic & Orthotic Services in York and South-Central PA - Aspire PO

Rabia Piracha speaker, relationships coach and entrepreneur.

Femala Fleming speaker, women's total fitness coach, and author of (your body is a multi-million-dollar corporation act like it).

Rhonda Y. Williams executive speak, coach, owner at above the grind leadership https://atgleadershipacademy.com/

Ryan Hartley mindset coach of conscious living Forward - Thinker's Life

Dee Rowan 2x author and motivational speaker

Ryan Rape thought leader, engineer, & animal advocate

Jeff Hancher keynote speaker, and host of (the champion forum).

Josh B Payne finance industry expert and speaker.

Pjero mardesic transformative therapist and business coach.

Coach DC physical fitness expert and speaker.

Lilly Wang Quantum success coach, spiritual consultant to entrepreneurs and speaker.

Lorna Green empowered mindset leader

Robynn Sheridan theta & akashic healing practitioner and thought leader.

Oracle Skai ascension coach/ quantum healer.

Michael Esguerra Certified Coach, Master Facilitator, Learning & Development inner peace Consultant https://www.mbelearning.com

Blessing to all in your tireless efforts to creating the best environments for people to live with a mindset of endless possibilities.

Shine on!

Inspired by Mom
Deacon Eva Laverne Miles~Rutledge